About the Author

Tamba Roy is an experienced Education Consultant and is also the Director of Trident Solutions. Trident Solutions provides powerful training events and workshops for Headteachers, school staff, parents and pupils. In addition to this, Tamba provides one to one coaching for school leaders, helping them to overcome challenges and experience even greater success. His experience includes: Headteacher of two schools, Senior Lecturer in Education Studies at Nottingham Trent University, Director of Formula 4 Educational Leadership, children's author, and Master Practitioner of Neuro-Linguistic Programming.

As a result of his outstanding leadership of a school, Tamba was invited to Downing Street in 2001 to meet with the Prime Minister and share insights with other successful leaders.

Since leaving his most recent Headship his work has focussed on developing practical techniques to help pupils to overcome the barriers limiting their achievement. 'Success in Schools' enables teachers, parents and carers to share these unique tools with children to support them in reaching their true potential.

Keynotes, Conferences, Training Days and Workshops

If you would like Tamba to lead an event, please contact the email address below. Similarly, if you have any specific comments about how you have used Success in Schools he would be delighted to hear from you.

Contact details:
Tamba Roy, Education Consultant
Trident Solutions www.trident-solutions.co.uk
e-mail: tamba@trident-solutions.co.uk

Success in Schools

A practical handbook of tools for teachers and parents to use with children.

Tamba Roy

Matador
9 Priory Business Park
Kibworth Beauchamp
Leicestershire LE8 0RX, UK
Tel: (+44) 116 279 2299
Fax: (+44) 116 279 2277
Email: books@troubador.co.uk
Web: www.troubador.co.uk/matador

ISBN 978 1780883 304

British Library Cataloguing in Publication Data.
A catalogue record for this book is available from the British Library.

Typeset in Calibri by Troubador Publishing Ltd
Printed and bound in Great Britain by Clays Ltd, St Ives plc

Matador is an imprint of Troubador Publishing Ltd

ACKNOWLEDGEMENTS

Considerable thanks go to my wife Gail for her professional insight and wonderful support. Also my appreciation goes to my sister Lucinda for her advice and expertise. Furthermore I must convey my gratitude to the many children, teachers and parents who have participated in the development of this book. An extra special 'thank you' goes to the children and staff at Mellors Primary School in Nottingham, Belmont Primary School in Derbyshire and Welbeck Primary School in Nottingham.

CONTENTS

Introduction

What is it?

Success in Schools will provide you with practical strategies and unique approaches that you can use to support the success of the children you work with if you are a teacher, or your own child/ren if you are a parent or carer.

My experience and knowledge comes from working with children and teachers for thirty years, including as the Headteacher of two schools and as a University Lecturer in Education Studies. For the last five years I have worked as an Education Consultant with my company Trident Solutions. The practical techniques within this book have been developed during my work with schools around the country.

As well as my experience within education, this book was inspired by a number of approaches, including 'Neuro-Linguistic Programming'. NLP was developed by Richard Bandler and John Grinder. They wanted to discover how exceptional individuals overcome barriers to experience success. They developed a highly successful strategy based on identifying patterns of behaviour that achieve outstanding results. NLP has been successfully used in business, sport and personal development for many years.

I have used my extensive experience as a Master Practitioner of NLP, as well as insights gained as a leader within education, to create the original set of tools within this handbook.

These tools have been specifically designed to enable teachers and parents to support the success of children in Primary and Secondary schools. They are all 'solution-focussed', which means that each tool can provide a unique solution to overcome a barrier. The provision of a clear outline for each of the techniques means that adults can easily and confidently share them with children. Once children are familiar with these tools, they can go on to use them without the need for adult support. This enables them to make more effective choices in their thinking, their behaviour and in their experience of success.

The Oxford English Dictionary defines success as: *"The accomplishment of an aim or purpose."* Any definition of success will link with achievement, but the focus will inevitably be subjective. Our personal view of success will depend upon our experiences, goals or desires. For children these might include: completing computer games; gaining the respect of peers; passing a test or exam; winning competitions; successful auditions and so on. Other successes we might wish for them would include: experiencing happiness; financial security; care and consideration of others; and achieving their potential. This book aims to provide solution-focussed approaches that will empower children to enjoy success both within school, and in their experiences throughout their lives.

The strategies incorporate a visualisation technique that helps to embed the process. When we close our eyes and visualise, brain scans reveal that parts of the brain respond as though we are actually engaged in that activity. In his international bestselling book 'The Brain that Changes Itself' Dr. Norman Doidge, psychiatrist and psychoanalyst, states: *"Imagining an act and doing it are not as different as they sound. When people close their eyes and visualise a simple object, such as the letter 'a', the primary visual cortex lights up, just as it would if the subjects were actually looking at the letter 'a'. Brain scans show that in action and imagination many of the same parts of the brain are activated. This is why visualising can improve performance."*

Why is this book important?

PROVIDES PRACTICAL TOOLS TO OVERCOME REAL CHALLENGES

Success in Schools contains a unique set of tools in the form of practical activities that can be used to support the success of children in all areas of life and learning. It provides a clear response to issues that can present challenges at school and at home every day, but which have in the past rarely been directly addressed.

Some of these issues relate to:

- focussing on success when writing or when completing a maths activity;
- dealing with a negative inner voice that can make children 'feel like a failure';

- 'letting go' of anxiety before a test, audition or exam;
- learning how to concentrate instead of being distracted;
- developing the resilience to deal with setbacks;
- helping children of exceptional ability to exceed their expectations.

DEVELOPS THE INDEPENDENCE OF CHILDREN

The solution-focussed tools within this book have not been created to give teachers or parents additional work. You already have enough to do! In fact, the aim of these approaches is to increase the independence of children by teaching them how to make effective choices. Then, as children become more engaged with learning and gain self esteem, they will feel empowered to take action to overcome challenges, giving teachers and parents, the time to focus on and enjoy their children's progress.

SUPPORTS POWERFUL HOME-SCHOOL LINKS

Success in Schools also provides a unique link between school and home. All of the activities within this handbook can be shared as easily at home as they can in the classroom. The clear guidelines for each tool, as well as the supportive follow-up activities, provide a basis for powerful positive dialogue between children, parents and teachers. Developing a strong partnership between teachers and parents has frequently been cited by the government as a major factor in raising pupil achievement.

PROMOTES LIFELONG SUCCESS IN AND OUT OF SCHOOL

The practical strategies within this book have the potential to support the success of children not only during their education, but for a lifetime. Many of the tools have been used to support leaders within education – for example, using 'Personal Power' before giving a major presentation, using 'Brilliant Breathing' to feel calmer when under pressure at work, or using 'Step Forward' to help determine and move towards inspirational goals.

How do you use this book?

Success in Schools contains fifteen approaches. The 'Which Tools When' section will help you to find the appropriate technique. The fifteen tools are divided into three phases with specific goals. The goals provide an opportunity to evaluate any new insights or changes in behaviour that may occur as a result of using the tools within the phase. However, the goals are only meant to be a guide, as the road to success is unique for each of us.

Each tool is explored under the following headings:

- *What is it?*
- *Why is this important?*
- *How do you do it? (Summary and The Full Script)*
- *When should I use it?*
- *Related Activities – Home*
- *Related Activities – School*

Each section contains relevant background information for teachers and parents, as well as full scripts that can be used directly with the children. These scripts will enable you to use the techniques confidently and effectively from the very first attempt. Use the scripts when you are new to these approaches because they are tried and tested, but once you gain experience don't be afraid to be creative in how you adapt the scripts.

When should you use this book?

You can dip into this handbook whenever children are facing a particular challenge, or you can use it as you would a training manual. For example, you might initially choose to share a new tool from phase one each week, in order to explore different ways of resolving problems and focussing on success. Once all the tools in the phase have been used and experienced, you can then evaluate the impact against the children's (or your) goals. This information will help you to decide whether to revisit some of the activities or to move on to phase two. Once all the tools in each phase have been introduced, children can then determine which one to use when they are faced with a barrier. Over time they should be encouraged re-visit the tools. This repetition helps to embed any new positive patterns of behaviour they have adopted.

The techniques are a flexible framework for success that will grow and develop as parents and teachers experience the positive impact they can have with children.

Caution

The tools within this book can have a powerful effect on the day-to-day challenges that children face, but as with any approaches aimed at supporting children, you should continue to follow the recommendations of any professionals who already work with your child. They will know his or her individual needs and requirements. I have deliberately designed these techniques to allow them to be used independently of, or alongside, other approaches. However, if you have any concerns whatsoever, or if your child is already receiving specific support or treatment, please consult the appropriate professional first.

The Drivers

You may find it helpful to read this section before using the tools. The Drivers described here will give you an understanding of the insights that underpin this book.

The Drivers are ten key tenets that are embedded within this book, which provide you with a greater understanding of the possibilities for success. Some of these original statements are adapted from what are known as the 'Presuppositions of Neuro-Linguistic Programming', and some are professional insights gained after working with children for many years as a senior leader in education.

1. "We are learning all day, every day!"

Children are incredibly successful at learning. They learn all the time.

*What, **all** the time?* Yes, all the time! On the surface this might not always be apparent – for example, when children still don't tidy their rooms despite repeated requests! However, all children are incredibly successful at learning. As humans, we cannot help but learn.

Daily life presents us with many opportunities for learning – for example:

> *Learning how to read.*
> *Learning how to ignore a headache.*
> *Learning how to 'get over' missing our favourite TV programme.*
> *Learning how to do a maths problem.*
> *Learning how to be patient with a brother or sister.*

However, what we learn may not be what was intended, or it may not be particularly beneficial! For example:

> *Learning to be angry.*
> *Learning to leave old plates of food under the bed.*

Learning to be anxious.
Learning to tease a younger sibling.

The trick is to match our choices and our patterns of behaviour so that this incredible ability to learn is linked with a quality outcome.

2. "The red box around us has an exit!"

We have certain beliefs about ourselves, and these can have a dramatic impact on our perceived success or failure. They can become the 'boxes' we place around ourselves that appear to define us. Sometimes these beliefs can support us – for example: *I've got a good imagination; I'm a good speller; I'm good at sport.*

However, sometimes our thoughts can limit us. I call these 'red box beliefs' – for example: *I'm no good at writing; I'll always be shy; I'll never be able to do that.*

These limiting self beliefs can have a dramatic impact on our self esteem and aspirations.

Success in Schools can provide the insight to recognise the 'box' *and* the key to unlock the exit.

(Of course, the 'box' doesn't need to be red – but it might be!)

3. "Mistakes are magnificent when they lead to learning."

Having the resilience to skilfully deal with setbacks is a key feature for long term success. The world's greatest advances only came about after many painstaking 'mistakes'. For instance, Thomas Edison was once asked how he felt after the thousands of failed attempts to make a bulb light up. He reportedly said, *"I didn't fail. I learned thousands of ways how **not** to make a bulb light up!"* Realising, that mistakes are an integral part of learning can dramatically alter how children view success or failure.

4. "We can always choose to have a choice."

In all that we do or experience, we can always choose to have a choice about how we respond. Sometimes our responses do not reflect real choice at all; rather, they are simply patterns of behaviour that we have consciously or sub-consciously learned. For example: when I think I might be late I become irritated; when I hand in a report I experience worry; when I speak in public I feel stressed, and so on. This book provides tools to help us understand that we have a choice, and that we can make effective choices.

5. "All decisions need action!"

We can decide to do many things, but unless we take action the decision will simply be a fantasy. For example, I might say *"I've decided to go to the gym"* – but I don't actually go! Or a child might say *"I've decided to do my homework"* – but the books remain unopened! Taking action is key, and this is our responsibility. This understanding allows us to have some control over our daily experiences, rather than simply being a victim of circumstance. If change is required, if the action is beneficial, and if it is not intended to have a negative impact on ourselves or others, then take action!

6. "Flexibility opens opportunities"

Teaching children to adapt to circumstances will give them the greatest chance for success. Encouraging children to be flexible in how they think and how they behave will allow them to move with the times and adapt to an ever-changing world. The most successful entrepreneurs practice this on a daily basis. It doesn't mean responding to every pressure, or changing who you are; but it does mean being flexible enough to make the most of each situation.

7. "We become experts at whatever we practice!"

This statement is often linked to achievements in sport, or professional qualifications, but it also includes frustration, hope, pessimism, anger, joy, frustration and so on. This is why some adults can become experts at getting angry when driving, and why some teenagers become outstandingly skilled at being bored, even when they're not! Adopting patterns of behaviour that allow us to excel can mean that experiencing success becomes a regular occurrence.

8. "Success is within us, and is always an option."

As soon as we are born we are inherently successful. We learn to observe, to copy, to differentiate, to have tenacity, to walk, to talk, and so on. We are born with the resources to succeed. However, challenging circumstances can mean that this natural ability to learn and succeed is replaced by doubt, fear of failure and a wide variety of limiting self-beliefs. When we understand that the skills to succeed are actually within us, and that what we need are the appropriate tools and support to access these inner resources, then we will realise that success is always an option.

9. "Rapport with others is very important. Rapport with ourselves is essential."
Helping children to have rapport with others will impact on all elements of their success. This doesn't mean 'agreeing with everyone'. Rather, it means giving children a platform for real communication by developing skills such as speaking, listening, and understanding non-verbal cues, as well as social skills that reflect empathy, tolerance and awareness.

Being 'in rapport with ourselves' is about experiencing a sense of balance. It's not about being selfish. We know that when we feel a sense of equilibrium, we are more likely to respond appropriately to those around us. Being 'in rapport with ourselves' includes being able to positively impact upon our own emotional state, to appreciate our accomplishments, and to enjoy our own company.

10. "The magic is in *this* moment."
This is the undeniable reality of every individual's existence. All that we do takes place within the narrow confines of the second just gone and the second that is to come. Focussing on this moment called 'now' can allow us to find a unique and profound space to relax, to reflect, to re-energise and – most importantly – not just to **be** successful but also **feel** successful!

Guide for sharing the scripts

For the sake of expediency the term 'children' is used throughout, although these guidelines are also for when you are sharing the scripts with one child.

1. Read through the script prior to use, to familiarise yourself with the content. *(As you gain confidence, feel free to amend and adapt the script.)*

2. If there are interruptions deal with them calmly, and then remind the children to re-focus and continue the activity. Don't worry if you have to stop altogether. Simply arrange to return to the activity another time.

3. Some scripts give guidance about delivery – for example, when to be slower and quieter, and when to be more energised. However, feel free to develop your own style as you share a script. (Don't worry if you feel a little nervous at first. The more you share the scripts, the more confident you will feel.)

4. If a tool requires a child to make a positive statement about themselves, for example, "I am successful", but they don't feel it or believe it yet, still encourage them to make the statement. By adopting new responses and new patterns of behaviour we can change our experiences, which can then provide evidence that can change our beliefs. However, if a child absolutely cannot make an affirming statement, don't force them. Simply carry on. (Of course, this is very useful information for you, because it will give you an indication of which tools you might use with this child to support positive self-esteem.)

5. All the children are asked to close their eyes when creating an outcome, because this helps to embed the process. However, if a particular child doesn't feel comfortable doing this, he or she can simply lower their eyes. Just remind them to be as still and as quiet as possible as they participate.

6. When you are using a tool together, develop the expectation in the children

that they will begin by looking at you and being still and quiet. *Some children who are very active might still need to move a little, or perhaps be given something to hold. (Although it's probably best that it's not something noisy!)* The great majority of children, especially ones who normally find 'being still' a challenge, frequently surprise teachers and parents with how focussed they can be when they are enjoying one of the tools.

If you are working with a class and there is a particular child who initially finds this too challenging, then plan for him or her to be with a colleague while you introduce the tool. When they return, the changed atmosphere in the class and the positive comments of the other children might well encourage the individual child to want to participate next time! (Of course, there are specific tools for children who believe they 'can't do it' or who choose not to join in, for example The Smasher or My Choice of Inner Voice.)

7. Occasionally children (and adults) might feel strong emotions when using the tools, for example, huge relief when they realise they're not alone in having a negative inner voice, or a sense of inadequacy if they find it hard to identify successes. If at any time a child feels very emotional and needs to feel calmer, sensitively lead him or her through Brilliant Breathing. (If appropriate you might then choose to address the particular issue, or to seek the advice of a teacher or another appropriate professional.)

8. Observe the children for non-verbal signs that reflect involvement.

   When using a script that encourages relaxation, possible signs to look for in the children might include:

   - stillness of body
   - stillness of face
   - being physically lower in their seat
   - giving the impression of slower, deeper breathing
   - head and body slightly downwards
   - taking several breaths to become 'fully alert' again afterwards
   - noticeably quieter and more focussed than before you read the script

   When the script supports an increase in energy or motivation, possible signs to look for in the children might include:

- facial reactions to the script even though the eyes are closed – for example, smiling
- the body making occasional small movements
- physically sitting more upright
- being quicker to 'come out' of the experience
- face and body more alert
- being more energised and ready to begin the next activity
- immediate comments about the activity when it finishes

9. When you become more confident at sharing a script, develop what I refer to as 'creative inclusion'. This is when we include interruptions as part of the script. Rather than trying to ignore potential distractions, this can be a powerful way to make the imagery even more tangible. For example, when a car is heard going past, it could be a reminder that they're moving quickly towards their goal. Similarly, when someone opens a door, it could be a reminder that they're opening doors to new possibilities. Don't feel you have to force creative inclusion, but if the opportunity arises, have fun with it!

10. Keep the whole activity as positive as possible, and most importantly, enjoy this unique time together.

Which Tools When?

The following three tables identify the fifteen tools and some of the areas they can support.

The tools are divided into phase one, phase two and phase three. The goals within these progressive phases provide an opportunity for you and your child(ren) to evaluate the learning and the overall experience.

Phase One

Tools	Objectives Teaching children how to...
Brilliant Breathing p. 21 Transforming our emotional state through breathing	• be still and focussed • let go of tension • feel more relaxed • calm down • take notice of breathing
Ready 4 Learning Ladder p. 27 Learning how to choose our own level of motivation	• concentrate for longer periods • feel more motivated when they don't feel inspired • realise their role in feeling motivated • participate in a fun activity to increase interest • enjoy learning
My Choice of Inner Voice p. 34 Changing our inner dialogue	• have a more positive response to experiences • respond appropriately to praise or compliments • make more effective choices about their behaviour • consider accepting success • develop greater patience
Personal Power p. 40 Creating inner strength and confidence	• feel more confident • feel more able to cope with change • recognise their own uniqueness • be more involved and pro-active • empower themselves
The Smasher p.46 Getting rid of a barrier	• get rid of a limiting belief about themselves • overcome barriers • identify the action they need to take • support others who need to feel successful • feel supported by peers

PHASE ONE GOALS

For children:
a) to understand that thoughts and feelings can be changed, and that they can influence their own success
b) to make use of the tools under the direction of an adult
c) to understand that different strategies can be used for different challenges
d) to be aware of changes they can make that will impact on their success at home or at school
e) to identify how some of the tools have impacted upon their experience of success

Phase Two	
Tools	**Objectives** **Teaching children how to...**
Shield p. 57 Creating a feeling of inner protection to support emotional resilience	• feel they have more options • recognise potential challenges • feel more confident • filter anticipated challenges • create a feeling of inner protection
Seeing Success p. 63 Creating a positive outcome	• change their view of a future event • recognise success • anticipate success • overcome setbacks • feel inspired to take action
Shrink p. 70 Letting go of barriers	• understand they have a choice • think creatively • let go of a fear or anxiety • share feelings with supportive peers • let go of a label
Personal Space p.76 Time to relax, reflect, re-energise	• reach a more sustained level of relaxation • focus on their visual, auditory and kinaesthetic awareness • think creatively • give themselves time and space • create a positive, inspirational place for themselves
The Jacket p.83 Developing resilience, recognising strengths	• recognise their own qualities and successes • feel they can change if they wish to do so • develop resilience and tenacity • recognise the qualities and successes of others • develop the impact of the Jacket with use

PHASE TWO GOALS

For children:
a) to show an awareness of thoughts or behaviours that help or hinder success
b) to use some of the tools effectively and independently
c) to make effective decisions about which strategies to use to support their success
d) to begin to exhibit new patterns of behaviour that help them to be successful
e) to evaluate their experiences and to learn from them

Phase Three

Tools	Objectives Teaching children how to...
Change Your Mind p.95 Seeing a solution rather than a problem	• realise they have a choice • notice the way they visualise a problem • focus on resolution • identify the solution to a problem • be pro-active
Step Forward p.101 Moving towards a powerful goal	• feel more connected to a goal • have fun 'experiencing' the future • develop greater motivation • create a more positive future for themselves • help others to aspire
Enjoying Excellence p.107 Exceeding expectations	• understand what is meant by excellence • recognise the qualities they have that can help them to achieve excellence • understand that excellence is linked with choice and action • understand that excellence is linked with a feeling • exceed their own expectations
Fab Future p.114 Consciously placing supportive goals into our future	• develop aspirations • consider a more positive perspective • feel they can influence their outcomes • question limits they have set themselves or others have 'given' to them • identify specific steps to success
Eye of the Storm p.121 Experiencing stillness	• feel calm under pressure • exhibit resilience • experience a deeper sense of self • appreciate the value of this moment • be prepared to succeed

PHASE THREE GOALS

For children:
a) to frequently make empowering choices that support their success
b) to use the tools proficiently, creatively and independently, adjusting them to match their particular needs
c) to have the skill, sensitivity and insight to advise others on how to experience success
d) to regularly **be** and **feel** successful
e) to be able to critically assess their own progress, and to skilfully act upon outcomes

THE PHASE ONE TOOLS

1. Brilliant Breathing
2. Ready 4 Learning Ladder
3. My Choice of Inner Voice
4. Personal Power
5. The Smasher

PHASE ONE GOALS

For children:

a to understand that thoughts and feelings can be changed, and that they can influence their own success

b to make use of the tools under the direction of an adult

c to understand that different strategies can be used for different challenges

d to be aware of changes they can make that will impact on their success at home or at school

e to identify how some of the tools have impacted upon their experience of success

TEACHING CHILDREN HOW TO:

- be still and focussed
- let go of tension
- feel more relaxed
- calm down
- take notice of breathing

Brilliant Breathing

Transforming our emotional state through breathing

"We are what we repeatedly do. Excellence then is not an act, but a habit."

Aristotle

WHAT IS IT?

Brilliant Breathing is a simple but powerful tool to share with children. It is a deep breathing technique that can enable them to change how they are feeling – for example, moving from anger to calm, or anxiety to relaxation.

When they experience this ability to alter their emotional state, it can open up a whole range of possibilities.

WHY IS THIS IMPORTANT?

- Brilliant Breathing can show children that they can influence how they feel.
- In a world that is moving faster and faster, Brilliant Breathing can help children to develop the 'art' of being still.

- It can be a lovely calming activity to share with a child at the end of the day.
- Once children are familiar with this tool they can use it anytime, anywhere to affect their emotional state.
- Brilliant Breathing turns the attention of the child inward, and is the first step to realising that *solutions can be within us, rather than always being outside us*.

HOW DO YOU DO IT?

Brilliant Breathing – Summary

1. Place one hand on your stomach.
2. Breathe out completely.
3. Slowly breathe in through your nose.
4. Breathe so that your hand moves and you notice your breath.
5. Stop for a second, and then let all the air flow smoothly and slowly out through your nose or mouth.
   You don't need to take in any extra breath to do this. Simply take normal breaths, but allow them to go all the way to your stomach.
6. Choose a colour that relaxes you and let this colour fill you with every breath you inhale.
7. Then, if you have a particular worry, imagine you are breathing it out every time you exhale.
8. So the pattern is – deep relaxed breathing, *breathe in* the calm colour and then *breathe out* the tension.

REACTIONS FROM CHILDREN WHEN USING BRILLIANT BREATHING

Whenever I visit schools, it is always very humorous when I ask children to breathe. Suddenly they act as though they've never done it before! Young children take in huge gulps of air, and older ones (and adults!) frequently start tensing their shoulders. When they concentrate on breathing for the first time they need a few moments to remember that they will succeed at this!

BRILLIANT BREATHING – THE SCRIPT:

Specific Delivery Style: Slow, relaxed pace.

HERE WE GO...

Today we're going to do an activity that you can then use whenever you want to feel calm. It's called Brilliant Breathing, and it can allow us to breathe in a way that helps us to relax, to unwind, or to be ready to do whatever we're going to do. Simply follow my instructions.

Remember what we do when we focus on success? Make sure your eyes are looking at me, you're listening very carefully, and your body is nice and still. Let's begin...

- Place one hand on your stomach.
- Breathe out completely.
- Breathe in through your nose so that the air makes your hand move.
- Stop for a second, and then quietly breathe out through your nose or mouth.
- Take another breath in, down to your stomach. Pause. Then quietly breathe out.
- And again. Breathe in down to your stomach. Pause. Then quietly breathe out.
- Now I'd like you to do this with your eyes closed and see if you notice any changes in how you are feeling. Close your eyes now.
- Place one hand on your stomach again. (Once they're confident about deep breathing you needn't worry about placing the hand on the stomach.)
- Breathe out completely.
- Breathe in through your nose so that your breath goes down to your stomach.
- Stop for a second, and then quietly breathe out through your nose or mouth.

- *You don't need to take in any extra breath to do this. Simply take normal breaths, but allow them to go all the way to your stomach.*

- *Remember to relax your shoulders as you do this. Sometimes we suddenly tense up when we realise we have to breathe! Don't worry, just let it flow naturally. The important thing is to allow the breath to go all the way to your stomach before you slowly breathe out.*

  (If a child feels a little light-headed it might be because he or she doesn't normally breathe this well, and they're not used to taking in so much oxygen. If necessary they can stop and relax, and then continue when they feel comfortable.)

- *As thoughts come into your head, smile (this shows you have an active mind!) and then just let the thoughts slip away as you focus on the breath again.*

- *Keep noticing your breath as you get better and better at this.*

- *Enjoy practising this deep breathing for a few moments.*

- *Now I'd like you to keep your eyes closed and choose a colour that will help you feel calm and happy. Go on, choose one right now – a colour that will help you to feel calm and happy. You don't need to tell me what it is. Just decide on a lovely relaxing colour. If you don't know what colour to choose, then imagine what colour you would choose if you did know.*

- *Now I want you to imagine that every time you breathe in, you are breathing in that colour. Do this right now. Notice how good it makes you feel. Notice that you can make that lovely colour fill you with every breath.*

- *As you breathe in, imagine that this lovely colour goes all the way around your body and right inside your head, giving you space to relax.*

- *Enjoy this for a few moments.*

- *Now I want you to remember how you feel when you are a bit worried. The worry might feel like a heaviness in your stomach, a tightness in your chest, or tangled 'spaghetti-thoughts' in your head.*

- *I want you to imagine that every time you breathe out, you are breathing out that worry feeling. Notice that this feels really nice. Notice that every breath out makes you feel lighter, as though you are letting go of a heavy bag you've been carrying. Enjoy this feeling for a few seconds.*

- *Keep your eyes closed, because now we're going to put it all together. Notice and enjoy your deep breathing, and practice breathing in the lovely colour and breathing out the worry feeling.*

- *I'm going to let you do this very quietly for a minute. See if you can notice the difference you have made to how you feel. Keep your eyes closed, breathe in the colour and breathe out the worry feeling. Breathe in the colour, breathe out the worry...*

  (If you feel confident you can lead their breathing, so they inhale and exhale in time to the words *Breathe in the colour, breathe out the worry...* Repeat as often as you wish.)

- *Keep going and I'll tell you when to stop...*

- *Take three more Brilliant Breaths and then open your eyes. Thank you. You've learned how to take action to help you to feel calmer.*

LEAD DRIVER

'The magic is in *this* moment' Being still and focussing on what is happening right *now* is a vital skill for children to learn. In a world that appears to be getting noisier and faster, this simple experience of a 'moment' can often have a profound impact on children (and adults).

WHEN SHOULD I USE IT?

Children At Home (Examples)

You might use it when your child:

- Is feeling tense or finds it hard to sleep
- Needs to unwind after watching TV or being on the computer
- Needs to have an immediate way to calm down after feeling upset

Children At School (Examples)

You might use it when children:

- Need to feel calmer
- Have witnessed a potentially stressful situation, for example, an accident or a bullying incident
- Have experienced some challenges at school, for example, preparing for a school play

RELATED ACTIVITIES AT HOME

1. Share Brilliant Breathing at bedtime to help your child sleep.
2. Enjoy experiencing Brilliant Breathing with your child, and talk about how you both felt. Share times when it might be useful to be able to relax and feel calm.
3. If you know of friends or family members who will positively participate, let your child teach them Brilliant Breathing.

RELATED ACTIVITIES AT SCHOOL

1. Ask the children to discuss how they feel before and after doing Brilliant Breathing, and list the emotions they experience.
2. Share ideas and make a display of different occasions when the children might use Brilliant Breathing.
3. Ask children to keep a log of the times when they've used Brilliant Breathing at school. Share this at the end of the day.

I JUST WONDERED...

What do you see, hear and feel when you are really still and quiet?

SOMETHING TO CONSIDER –THE IMPORTANCE OF A BREATH

The importance of focussed breathing should not be under-estimated. If we practice deep breathing we will stimulate a calmer, more balanced response in everything we do, and recent research suggests regular practice may have even wider implications. Deep breathing brings vital oxygen to our bodies, which means that our hearts do not have to work so hard. The thirty-year-long Framingham Heart Study, conducted in the US, has identified that most of the human nervous system reacts to how we take in a breath. Research suggests that the most significant factor in health and longevity is how well we breathe!

TEACHING CHILDREN HOW TO:

- concentrate for longer periods
- feel more motivated when they don't feel inspired
- realise their role in feeling motivated
- participate in a fun activity to increase interest
- enjoy learning

Ready 4 Learning Ladder

Learning how to choose our own level of motivation

"The greatest discovery of my generation is that a man can alter his life by altering his attitudes."
William James, 1842–1910

WHAT IS IT?

Ready 4 Learning Ladder is a tool that can help children to feel more engaged in learning. It encourages them to take a measure of responsibility for their level of motivation.

WHY IS THIS IMPORTANT?

- Ready 4 Learning Ladder can help children to take control of their level of motivation and put them in a more empowered state for learning.
- Rather than focussing on external factors – for example, the 'excitement' of the activity – this tool has the unique approach of focussing on how children feel inside themselves.

- It can be a fun approach to share with children, as they can have 'competitions' to see who can get really motivated!

HOW DO YOU DO IT?

Ready 4 Learning Ladder – Summary

1. Imagine a ladder in front of you that is twice your height.
2. The top of the ladder says one hundred, and the bottom of the ladder says zero.
3. All the numbers from zero to one hundred are on the ladder.
4. Zero, at the bottom, is when you are finding it hard to feel motivated. One hundred, at the top, is when you are REALLY ready to learn!
5. Close your eyes and look at the number you feel you are at right now.
6. Notice that as you move up the ladder you **see** yourself looking more motivated.
7. Notice that as you move up the ladder you **hear** your inner voice saying 'I can do this'.
8. Notice that as you move up the ladder you **feel** increasingly confident in your ability to take action.
9. See how motivated you choose to be as you move up the ladder.
10. Have fun changing your level of motivation by moving up or down the ladder.

REACTIONS FROM CHILDREN WHEN USING READY 4 LEARNING LADDER

I've got to move! Although the following script encourages the children to 'look' up and down the ladder, don't be surprised if you see some individuals moving their arms or legs! Some children who are very kinaesthetic, automatically imagine that they are literally climbing up and down the ladder!

READY 4 LEARNING LADDER – THE SCRIPT

Specific Delivery Style: Energy, pace and definitely enthusiastic!

Today we're going to do an activity that we can use whenever we don't feel like doing something, or we feel bored, or we can't concentrate. Imagine if we could make ourselves feel excited about something we normally feel fed up about! Would that be a useful thing to be able to do?

This activity is called Ready 4 Learning Ladder, and it can allow us to notice that we can change our feelings about anything we are asked to do. The more you can join in and enjoy doing this, the more powerful it can be!

Remember what we do when we focus on success? You make sure your eyes are looking at me, you're listening very carefully, and your body is nice and still. Let's begin...

- *We'll start by Brilliant Breathing, but instead of focussing on relaxation, this time we're going to focus on feeling energised. Imagine that each breath you take in allows you to feel more alert and focussed. Each breath out takes away any tiredness. So it's **breathe in –energy; breathe out –tiredness.*** (Repeat as often as you wish as you model the breathing.)

- *Make this so clear that you notice yourself feeling more alert than you were a few moments ago.*

- *Make this so clear that even I can see you're more energised!*

- *Good. Now I'd like you to imagine there is a ladder in front of you, which is twice as tall as you are. Yes, imagine a ladder right in front of you!*

- *Decide what it is made of. Plastic? Wood? Metal?*

- *Put your hand up when you've chosen a colour for the ladder.* (This is useful information because you can see how quickly the children are fully participating.)

- *I want you to notice that the numbers zero to one hundred go up the ladder.*

- *Right at the bottom of the ladder it says zero.*

- *Right at the top of the ladder you see the number one hundred. Well done.* (If you are using this exercise with younger children, use the numbers one to twenty if necessary.)

- *Zero is when you feel really bored! Show me what your face and body look like when you are **really** bored!* (At this point you hope they move!) *Gosh! Very convincing!*

- *One hundred is when you are excited and really ready to begin learning. Show me what your face and body look like when you are **really** excited! Excellent!*

- *Now take a really good look at the ladder. Notice the numbers, starting at zero at the very bottom, right up to one hundred at the very top.*

- *Imagine you can see the number that shows how you feel right now. Remember, the lower the number, the more bored you feel. The higher the number, the more interested you feel. Put your hand up when you can see the number.* (At this point it can be very interesting to hear their numbers!)

- *Now I want you to close your eyes and notice that as you look up to the higher numbers you become even more interested!*

- *Notice that as you look higher up the ladder you **see** yourself looking upwards, and you're more confident.*

- *Notice that as you look higher up the ladder you **hear** your inner voice saying 'I can do this!'*

- *Notice that as you look higher up the ladder you **feel** motivated, and this makes you sit up straight with a smile on your face!*

- *Now I want you to keep your eyes closed, but we're going to have fun with this. We're going to move from number to number. See how fantastically you can change how you feel! The lower the number, the more bored you feel. The higher the number, the more excited and ready you feel. I'll be able to tell just by looking at you!*

- *Move right down to four. Notice how it feels. Are you **really** bored?* (Encourage them to reply in a **really** bored way!)

- *Move up to twenty-five. Notice how it feels? Still a bit bored?*

- *Move up higher to fifty-four. Notice how it feels. Ok?*

- *Move up even higher, to seventy-seven. Notice how it feels. Pretty good?*

- *Move all the way up to ninety-nine! Excellent! Open your eyes! Have you chosen to make yourselves really motivated? (The word 'chosen' is important here. They need to know that they have the power to do this if they choose to.) Well done.*

- *When you next feel a bit bored, have fun changing your level of motivation by focussing on the Ready 4 Learning Ladder, and then notice the difference you have made to how you feel.*

- *The more you practice this, the easier it becomes. Enjoy!*

   (A fun extension activity is to have the children sit in pairs and call out a motivation number for their partner to 'reach'!)

LEAD DRIVER

'We can always choose to have a choice!' – Ready 4 Learning Ladder can encourage us to make choices that support our success, even when we don't feel that inspired.

WHEN SHOULD I USE IT?

Children at Home (Examples)

You might use it when your child:
- Needs to have a strategy to get out of bed and get ready
- 'Can't be bothered' to do something
- Is procrastinating about homework

Children At School (Examples)

You might use it when children:
- Are about to start a lesson and you want to gauge the level of motivation
- Appear to lack energy and enthusiasm
- Need to understand that they also have a part to play in feeling motivated

RELATED ACTIVITIES – HOME

1. Talk with your child about when she or he feels bored or motivated. What's the first sign of boredom? For example, it might be looking miserable, sighing, sitting low in the seat and feeling 'weighed down', and so on. How could they change this pattern? For example, by smiling, physically move positions, sitting upright, putting on some great music, thinking of something they're looking forward to.

2. Share times when you've felt really motivated when you've been learning something. For example, you might talk about your favourite subject at school, playing a sport, riding a bike and so on. How did you know you were motivated?

3. Have fun by asking your child to use Ready 4 Learning Ladder with you. They call out a number, and you instantly change your level of 'motivation'. (Zero is really bored and one hundred is really interested.) What differences do they notice?

RELATED ACTIVITIES – SCHOOL

1. Create a model of a Ready 4 Learning Ladder that you can have at the front of the classroom. (Have fun using this during lessons.)

2. Discussion: How did they feel when they were at zero or one hundred? How could they make use of this? (If any children say they felt 'the same', ask them to think of a time when they felt really motivated. For example, you might suggest, really enjoying a sport, waking up on their birthday, or winning a computer game. Then ask them to imagine that feeling right now, because that's probably pretty close to one hundred!)

3. Ask the children to make a list of three times when they have felt really motivated. What did they see, hear and feel during each of these times? Allow the children to share these, and embed the good feelings by getting the rest of the class to cheer. Ask the child to imagine that these positive feelings have been attached to the number one hundred. This 'anchor' can help children to instantly access that positive state when they next think of the number one hundred on the Ready 4 Learning Ladder.

I JUST WONDERED...

What will you do differently, now you can choose to become really motivated?

SOMETHING TO CONSIDER – 'VAK'

The majority of children will have greater concentration when the activity relates to their dominant style of learning – visual, auditory or kinaesthetic or preferably all three! However, this cannot always be the case, and some activities will inevitably be less stimulating than others. Neuro-Linguistic Programming has shown that we can change our own response patterns if we are feeling bored. We can feel more positive by being more physically alert, and by visualising what we will see, hear and feel when we are truly motivated.

TEACHING CHILDREN HOW TO:

- have a more positive response to experiences
- respond appropriately to praise or compliments
- make more effective choices about their behaviour
- consider accepting success
- develop greater patience

My Choice of Inner Voice

Changing our inner dialogue

"If we want children to develop positive self-esteem, we have to show them that however young they are, they are capable of decisions that have an impact on their own experiences and their own lives."
Julie Fisher – Starting from the Child

WHAT IS IT?

This technique focusses on the voice inside a child's head. Sometimes the inner dialogue can be very supportive, encouraging or motivating the child, but sometimes it can create huge barriers and lead children to misinterpret their experiences.

It's important to point out that this voice is often strongly linked to vivid visual images or very specific feelings. My Choice of Inner Voice aims to impact upon visual, auditory and kinaesthetic awareness.

WHY IS THIS IMPORTANT?

- At times all children feel low self worth, and the inner dialogue that might accompany this can be damaging. My Choice of Inner Voice encourages them to take control of the words used and the feelings created by their inner dialogue, and to set up new patterns of possibilities.

- We rarely discuss the inner voice with children. This is a serious oversight that can make them feel that their internal dialogue is unusual or strange!
- Discussing the inner dialogue can provide tremendous insight into how children think.

HOW DO YOU DO IT?

(Resources for each child: Large piece of paper, felt pens or crayons)

My Choice of Inner Voice – Summary

1. Learn to notice what your inner voice says when you are asked to do something that might be challenging.
2. Notice whether, in your mind, you see yourself succeeding or failing. (SEE)
3. Are the words in your inner dialogue supportive or negative? (HEAR)
4. Notice if the feeling in your stomach is closer to nervousness or excitement. (FEELING)
5. Each time you notice your inner voice making you feel unhappy, replace the comment with a Power Statement. These are words that empower and support you. (*Even if you don't initially believe the affirming statement, it can be a first step to changing a pattern of low self belief.*)
6. Write down your Power Statement.
7. Repeat your Power Statement five times inside your head.
8. Call out the Power Statement, making sure you are looking confident and powerful.
9. Practice using the Power Statement so you really notice a difference in how you are feeling.

REACTIONS FROM CHILDREN WHEN USING MY CHOICE OF INNER VOICE

Some children have stated that their inner voice not only makes negative comments, but does so in a really harsh or aggressive tone of voice. Changing the tone, pace or volume of the inner voice can produce interesting results. Even changing the voice to that of a cartoon or television character can alter the negative impact.

MY CHOICE OF INNER VOICE – THE SCRIPT

(Resources: Large piece of paper, felt pens or crayons)

We're going to do a fun activity called My Choice of Inner Voice.

Did you know that we all have a voice inside our heads? Every time we do anything, the inner voice will have a comment about it. It might say 'Great!' or 'I can do this!' or simply 'Yes!' But it might also make us feel fed up, or believe that we won't be much good at something. It might say 'I'll be rubbish at this', 'I'm useless at drawing' or perhaps 'They won't like me'.

My Choice of Inner Voice helps us to choose an inner voice that supports us and helps us to do what we need to do.

Remember what we do when we focus on success? You make sure your eyes are looking at me, you're listening very carefully, and your body is nice and still. Let's begin...

- *I'd like you to start by Brilliant Breathing. Take in nice easy breaths and allow the air to go right to your stomach before you slowly breathe out.*

- *As you do this, relax your shoulders.*

- *I want you to think about the voice inside your head. Think about whether this voice generally makes you feel good or bad.*

- *Put your hand up if it generally makes you feel good. Thanks, put your hands down.*

- *Put your hand up if it generally makes you feel bad. Thanks, put your hands down.*

- *Put your hand up if you don't know. Thanks, put your hands down.*

- *Now I want you to imagine that you've been asked to do something that you think you might find hard to do – for example, speak in front of the whole school.*

- *Notice what your inner voice is saying to you about this challenge. In a minute I'll ask you to share some of your responses.*

- *If you can imagine how this will turn out, do you see it going well or going badly?* **(SEE)**

- *If there are words inside your head, are they helpful or not?* **(HEAR)**

- *If there's a feeling in your stomach, does it make you feel excited or nervous?* **(FEEL)**

- *Put your hand up if you would like to share how it makes you feel.*

- *From now on, each time you notice your inner voice making you feel bad, change the words to a Power Statement.*

- *A Power Statement might be a word or a sentence that makes you feel more confident, so that you can have a go and do your best.*

    For example, your Power Statement might be:

    > **'Yes!'**

    > *or* **'I'm learning all the time!'**

    > *or* **'Wow!'**

    > *or* **'I can do this!'**

- *Right now, I want you to choose your own Power Statement. Make it one that will really help* **you.** (If it will help, have some examples on display for the children to look at.)

- *Even if at the moment you find it hard to believe the statement, I want you to really imagine that you do.*

    I'll give you a moment to do this...

- *Thank you. Now I would like you to write down your Power Statement in big letters on the paper in front of you. Colour the background in a dark colour, and colour the words in a bright colour. Make sure they really stand out.* (This helps to embed their statements in their minds.)

- *Now I'd like you to close your eyes.*

- *I want you to imagine you can see yourself looking really confident. I'll be able to tell if you're doing this by looking at your face, your smile and how upright you're sitting.*

- *Say your Power Statement five times really loudly* **inside your head**, *and hold up your fingers so that I can see you counting as you do this. Off you go.*

- *Now sit up straight. Look at me, and when I say one two three go, I want you to call your Power Statement out loud so that I can hear it. Ready? One, two, three, go!* (Even though individual words or phrases may well be lost, the power of the statements should be very evident!) *Wow!*

- *From now on you can say your Power Statement to yourself whenever you notice your inner voice making you feel bad. I want you to do this loudly, but inside your head so nobody else can hear it.*

- *The more you remember to do this, the more you will notice that you can have your choice of inner voice! Well done! You've created a powerful way to support yourself.*

LEAD DRIVER

'The red box around us has an exit' If we can learn to influence our inner voice we can get past one of our biggest barriers to success.

WHEN SHOULD I USE IT?

Children At Home (Examples)

You might use it when your child:
- Has an internal dialogue which is generally a 'foe' rather than a 'friend'
- Feels 'stupid'
- Has got homework and keeps procrastinating

Children At School (Examples)

You might use it when children:
- Are worried about asking or answering a question
- Feel they can never be clever
- Find it hard to accept praise

Useful 'tests' **– How does your child react when he or she:**
- Is asked to complete a new challenge?
- Has made a mistake?
- Loses during a game?
- Is given a compliment?
- Is asked to share something with peers?
- Looks in the mirror?
- Has to do something independently?

RELATED ACTIVITIES AT HOME

1. Talk with your child about the voice inside our heads. (Share the fact that we all have an inner voice and sometimes it helps us, but sometimes it can get in the way.)
2. Laugh about the inner voice and how it can make us all behave in a silly way at times!
3. Ask your child what Power Statement she or he is going to use. (This should be a supportive word or phrase that can replace a negative inner comment.)

RELATED ACTIVITIES AT SCHOOL

1. At the beginning of a new activity, ask the children to share the comments from their inner voice.
2. Ask the children to create an image of their inner voice – for example, a 'creature', an animal or a face – and discuss what inspired them.
3. Make a display of the Power Statements that each child has created to support him or herself. (Each child could create two or three Power Statements which could then be used to support them in a range of situations.)

I JUST WONDERED...

Do you notice when your inner voice is being unreasonably negative, and do you realise you have the power to change this?

SOMETHING TO CONSIDER – 'OUR CLOSEST COMPANION'

We rarely discuss internal dialogues with children, and yet in many ways their inner voice is their 'closest companion'. The inner voice can be a child's greatest ally, but it can also be one of the biggest barriers they will ever face. It may be the thing that helps them to fly, or the thing that literally stops them in their tracks. Understanding that it is *their* voice and that they can influence it can be a revelation, and may dramatically support a child's experience of success.

Personal Power

Creating inner strength and confidence

"Athletes have understood for a long time that muscles are affected by visualisation and therefore mentally see themselves achieving at the highest level."
David R. Hamilton PhD – *Mind and Body*

WHAT IS IT?

Personal Power is a technique that can help children to create a more self assured, empowered emotional state. It encourages them to change themselves from the inside out, rather than always looking to other people or other things to make them feel better. There's more to us than meets the eye, and Personal Power can help children to tap into these inner resources.

WHY IS THIS IMPORTANT?

- At times, all children lack the confidence or fortitude to do something. Personal Power can help to counteract this by providing a focussed structure for changing how they feel inside.

- Personal Power is about attaining balance. It's not about being self absorbed or feeling superior. When children are 'out of balance', even the tiniest things can cause them to treat themselves or others negatively. When they are 'in balance', they feel more inclined to deal with themselves and others appropriately.
- Personal Power is a tool that the children themselves control, so that they are not so reliant on an adult to make the difference.
- Personal Power can help to give children the motivation to take action.

HOW DO YOU DO IT?

Personal Power - Summary

1. Close your eyes and imagine you can see a beautiful image or symbol shining in the middle of your stomach. This could be a lovely shape, a star, a light or whatever you like.
2. What colour is this image?
3. What sounds does it have? Swishing? Sizzling? Like a beautiful firework?
4. What feelings does it bring? Warmth? Joy? Confidence?
5. Close your eyes and allow the colour, the sounds and the feelings to fill your body, your arms, your legs and lastly your head.
6. Notice the positive differences you are choosing to make.
7. Now 'turn up' the colours, the sounds and the fantastic feelings until you really notice the changes you have made.

REACTIONS FROM CHILDREN WHEN USING PERSONAL POWER

I love using this tool with individuals or very large groups of children. It's great fun to observe them 'turning up' the brightness, the sounds and the feelings and seeing the children becoming more physically upright, more energised and more confident.

PERSONAL POWER – THE SCRIPT

Specific Delivery Style: Energy, pace and enthusiasm

Today we're going to find some Personal Power! This means that we're going to do an activity that can help us to feel much more confident whenever we wish. Sounds good, doesn't it? Personal Power is a way to make us see, hear and feel better than we did. It's great fun to do.

Remember what we do when we focus on success? You make sure your eyes are looking at me, you're listening very carefully, and your body is nice and still. Let's begin...

- *Everyone sit up straight.*

- *Right. Are you all ready for this?*

- *Let's begin by Brilliant Breathing. Breathe in and let the air go right down to your stomach. Stop for two seconds and then slowly and quietly breathe out. Enjoy this feeling.*

- *I want you to imagine that every breath you take in makes you feel really powerful!*

- *I want you to imagine that every breath you take in makes you feel really confident!*

- *I want you to imagine that every breath you take in makes you feel ready for anything!*

- *I want you to notice that your body feels ready to enjoy Personal Power!*

- *I want you to notice that your mind feels ready to enjoy Personal Power!*

- *Are you all really ready?* (Make sure you get a VERY positive response!)

- *Brilliant! Now I want you close your eyes and picture a tiny bright shining image. It could be a shape, it could be a cloud, it could be a bright light, it could be a star. Whatever it is, make sure you choose something that you can imagine getting brighter and brighter! If you can't decide, just choose whatever bright, positive shining image you can think of right now. Good.*

- *Now comes the powerful part! Keep your eyes closed and imagine you can see this wonderful tiny shining image, right in the middle of your stomach. Use your brilliant imagination to picture it really clearly.*

- *Give this image a bright powerful colour! Make it a colour that you really like and which will make you feel great. Keep your eyes closed and enjoy this lovely colour.*

- *Now I want you to give this image a sound. Make it a sound that makes you feel really powerful. Maybe a sparkling sound, or a sound like a fantastic firework. Keep your eyes closed and enjoy this incredible sound.*

- *Now I want you to give this image a feeling. This should be a feeling that makes you feel really confident. Maybe how you feel when you win a game, or how you feel when you help a friend. Keep your eyes closed and enjoy this fantastic feeling. If you find this hard, then imagine the feeling you might get when you complete an incredibly hard level on a computer game, or when you finish drawing the best picture you have ever done.*

- *Imagine you can see, hear and feel this image right now.*

- *Keep your eyes closed and allow the colour to fill your body, your arms, your legs and your head.*

- *Keep your eyes closed and hear the sound getting louder and more beautiful.*

- *Keep your eyes closed and notice that this lovely feeling is even better.*

- *Allow this shining, colourful feeling to flow around your body; especially your chest. Notice how powerful you feel.*

- *Allow this shining, colourful feeling to flow around your head. Notice how wonderful you feel.*

- *You've done really well, but your image could shine even brighter, sound even more sparkly, feel even more amazing! Imagine it is on number five, and I want you to turn it up to number seven. Go on, right now, turn it up to seven! Excellent!*

- *Now let's make it even stronger! Turn it right up to number nine. Wow! I can tell by looking at you that you're feeling more confident!*

- *Now I know this is risky, but let's turn it up all the way to number ten! Go on, right now. Turn it up to the max!*

- *Fantastic! Notice that you've taken control and chosen to feel more confident. You can use this tool whenever you need to feel stronger inside yourself.*

- *Finally, I'd like you to take three brilliant breaths, smile at your success, and open your eyes. Thank you.*

LEAD DRIVER

'Success is within us and is always an option!' – Personal Power can help us to appreciate ourselves by recognising the inner resources that we all carry with us.

WHEN SHOULD I USE IT?

Children at Home (Examples)

You might use it when your child:
- Is worried about sleeping in the dark
- Is worried about an audition or a competition
- Feels unsure about a physical activity, for example, swimming, gymnastics, a team game etc.

Children at School (Examples)

You might use it when children:
- Are worried about a test or performance
- Feel anxious about playtimes
- Feel ill-equipped to cope with change

RELATED ACTIVITIES AT HOME

1. Talk with your child about some times when they might feel the need to use Personal Power.
2. Discuss the Personal Power symbol they would like to have – for example, they might choose a shining star, a mythical animal, a cloud... Discover why they chose this.
3. Ask your child how she or he feels when they are REALLY confident! What is different?

I JUST WONDERED...

What would you do if you couldn't fail?

SOMETHING TO CONSIDER – 'CAUSE' OR 'EFFECT'?

Did you know that one of the greatest causes of stress in children and adults is the feeling that we don't have any control over what is happening to us? We sometimes believe we have little power or few choices. In Neuro-Linguistic Programming this is often spoken about in terms of 'cause' and 'effect'. When we believe things just 'happen to us', we can feel we are stuck on the 'effect' side of the equation. When we have some element of influence and control we feel we have options, and we tend to feel we are on the 'cause' side of the equation. The techniques within this book can help us to move from feeling we lack choices, (the effect side), to feeling we can make choices, (the cause side) and to take appropriate action.

TEACHING CHILDREN HOW TO:

- get rid of a limiting belief about themselves
- overcome barriers
- identify the action they need to take
- support others who need to feel successful
- feel supported by peers

The Smasher

Getting rid of a barrier

"The clever know what to learn. The wise know what to unlearn" T.Roy

WHAT IS IT?

All children face challenges. Sometimes these are linked with what I call 'barrier learning' – for example, learning to expect failure, learning to ignore aspirations, or learning to be bored. These can be huge obstacles for children, and their imaginations can make the problems even more daunting. However they can also use their vivid imaginations to help them overcome these challenges. The Smasher provides an exciting structure for doing just that!

WHY IS THIS IMPORTANT?

- This fun activity can provide a powerful insight into how children view the challenges they face.
- The collaborative nature of The Smasher can provide children with unique support from adults or peers.
- Children can smash barriers without even identifying them to anyone else!

The child can choose an image or words that mean something to them, but not to others.

HOW DO YOU DO IT?
(Resources: Pencil and paper)

The Smasher - Summary

1. Imagine a wall in front of you.
2. On this wall, written in big letters, are beliefs that are holding you back. For example, these might be "I'm shy", "I'm no good at writing", or "I'm not clever".
3. Write these words down on a piece of paper
4. Now, imagine that just above the wall there is a huge concrete ball attached to a chain, with a handle and a big red switch.
5. You turn the handle ten times and make the ball go higher and higher above the wall.
6. Count out loud from ten down to one, and then press the red switch.
7. The ball hurtles down and smashes the wall to smithereens!
8. When the dust clears, the wall and all the obstacles have completely gone!

REACTIONS FROM CHILDREN WHEN USING THE SMASHER

This activity normally ends with laughter and exclamations! The vocal countdown and the powerful visual imagery make it a favourite with children. If you aim to have as much fun as you can when sharing the script, you will see this reflected in the engagement of children and the depth of their responses.

THE SMASHER – THE SCRIPT

Resources: Paper and pencil
Specific Delivery Style: Energy and enjoyment!

Now we're going to use The Smasher! Any idea what this could be? (Share responses if you wish.)

In fact, The Smasher is a great way to change how we feel about something. Using this technique we can completely smash an old belief about ourselves that is holding us back. What's really fun about this is that we can do this together, and we can help each other to make this change happen.

Remember what we do when we focus on success? You make sure your eyes are looking at me, you're listening very carefully, and your body is nice and still. Let's begin...

- *I want you to begin by choosing something that you think you can't do very well, or something you believe about yourself that you're not happy with. For example, you might choose "I'm too shy", or "I'm no good at writing", or "I can't do Maths".*

  For now, choose something that you don't mind sharing. (When children are familiar with the technique they can use it themselves, if they don't want to share.)

- *Now be very clear about what the problem is. For example, if you feel shy you might say, "I'm too shy to make friends when I don't know anyone". If you think you're no good at writing you might say, "I can't think of what to write when we do stories." If you think you can't do Maths you might say, "I can never remember how to do fractions."*

- *Write these words down on a piece of paper. (Give them enough time and support to identify their barriers.)*

- *Thank you. Now I want you to close your eyes and imagine that your words are written in big letters on a high brick wall.*

- *Imagine you are standing next to the wall. What can you **see**? What colour is the wall? How big are the letters? What colour are they? (Share responses.)*

- *What can you **hear**? What does the voice inside your head say about this? (Share responses.)*

- *What do you **feel** when you imagine the wall and the writing? (Share responses.)*

- *Now, imagine that just above the wall there is a huge concrete ball hanging from a chain. There is also a big handle that raises the chain.*

- *Further away from the wall you see a bright red switch, with a notice that says 'Press this and the huge concrete ball will drop!'*

- *Imagine that you have the incredible strength to turn the handle and make the ball go higher and higher above the wall. As we count out loud from one to ten, use all your super strength to turn the handle ten times. I want to be able to see that the handle is heavy! Ready? **One, two, three, four, five, six, seven, eight, nine, ten.***

- *Great! The huge concrete ball is high above the wall that has held you back for so long.*

- *Now I want you to remind me of the words that are on your wall. These are the words you're going to smash! The words hold a belief that you're going to get rid of today! Could you all call out those words right now?*

- *Brilliant! Now it's time to smash that wall!*

- *Here we go! We're going to count out loud from ten to one, and then we're all going to press the red switch. When we do, we will all make a huge crashing sound! Ready? **Ten, nine, eight, seven, six, five, four, three, two, one**. NOW!*

- *The dust clears, and you see that the wall that was holding you back has completely gone. Phew!*

- *I want you to notice how different you feel!*

- *Notice how you feel now that you've chosen to completely destroy that old belief! And remember – that belief you used to have has turned to dust. It's gone – forever! If you ever feel that it might come back, change your inner voice and remember the strength you showed when you smashed that wall to smithereens!*

- *Now, tell me what's changed for you now that you have smashed that belief into dust. What's the first thing you will do differently now? (Share responses.)*

- *Well done for choosing to make such a powerful change to how you feel.*

LEAD DRIVER

'The red box around us has an exit!' – The Smasher directly challenges any limiting self beliefs and provides a way forward that is full of possibilities.

WHEN SHOULD I USE IT?

Children At Home (Examples)

You might use it when your child:
- Believes he or she can't make friends
- Thinks he or she is 'stupid'
- Can't forgive him or herself for making a big mistake

Children At School (Examples)
You might use it when children:
- Think they are 'rubbish' at reading, writing etc.
- Think they can't be successful
- Feel too worried about a sports activity to 'have a go'

RELATED ACTIVITIES AT HOME

1. Talk with your child about how she or he felt when the barrier was smashed. What will this do for them?
2. Next time you are with your child and you see a crane, remind him or her of the huge barrier they 'smashed'.
3. Together with your child, draw a picture or make a model of The Smasher and share times when you might use it.

RELATED ACTIVITIES AT SCHOOL

1. On a display board, create a background of a 'broken' wall and display the children's smashed 'limiting self beliefs'.
2. In assembly, have the children teach the rest of the school about The Smasher and how to use it. (This is very powerful when all the children are supporting each other and counting together.)
3. Have a discussion with the children identifying how they can support each other when they've smashed a barrier to make sure it stays 'smashed'.

At a later date if similar issues arise, you can remind the children of the powerful strength they showed when they chose to smash that barrier, and how much better they felt afterwards. *(If necessary, encourage them to remember clearly and **feel** that empowered state.)*

I JUST WONDERED...

What can you do to make sure that the barrier you have 'smashed' stays smashed?

SOMETHING TO CONSIDER – COMPLIMENTS

Our opinion of ourselves can sometimes be a huge barrier to feeling successful. An interesting question is '*What do you do with compliments?*' Do you enjoy and accept them? Or do you ignore them, disbelieve them, feel you must immediately 'say something nice back', turn them into a joke, or simply think the person is lying to be kind? Learning to respond by looking the person in the eye, smiling and simply saying 'thank you' can be a powerful catalyst for positive change.

THE PHASE TWO TOOLS

1.   Shield
2.   Seeing Success
3.   Shrink
4.   Personal Space
5.   The Jacket

PHASE TWO GOALS

For children:

a. to show an awareness of thoughts or behaviours that help or hinder success
b. to use some of the tools effectively and independently
c. to make effective decisions about which strategies to use to support their success
d. to begin to exhibit new patterns of behaviour that help them to be successful
e. to evaluate their experiences and to learn from these

TEACHING CHILDREN HOW TO:

- feel they have more options
- recognise potential challenges
- feel more confident
- choose to filter anticipated challenges
- create a feeling of inner protection

Shield

Creating a feeling of inner protection to support emotional resilience

"... having hope means that one will not give in to overwhelming anxiety, a defeatist attitude, or depression in the face of difficult challenges or setbacks."
Daniel Goleman – Emotional Intelligence

WHAT IS IT?

Shield is a way for children to feel stronger when faced with a challenge. It is a simple strategy for anchoring themselves into a more empowered state of awareness, which can make them feel less vulnerable and more able to experience success.

WHY IS THIS IMPORTANT?

- Shield can help children to feel more emotionally resilient when faced with challenges.
- It can encourage them to ask for help.

- Children can begin to recognise their inner resources.
- Shield can be just enough to give children a 'breathing space' to consider how they might overcome the problem – for example, by sharing it with a trusted adult.

HOW DO YOU DO IT?
(Resources: Paper, pencil, colours)

Shield - Summary

1. Draw a picture of yourself.
2. Draw a problem you are facing.
3. Choose a colour that makes you feel protected, and colour all around the picture of you.
4. Close your eyes, and during the count from one to five imagine a positive colour, a sound and a feeling that surrounds you.
5. Now notice that the problem CANNOT get past your shield!
6. It tries three times to get past, but it just bounces off further away each time!
7. Choose a small physical action that 'activates' your shield, so that you notice the difference.
8. Now you can use this extra confidence whenever you need to – for example, to tell a teacher or a parent about the problem you are worried about, so that they can help you.

REACTIONS FROM CHILDREN WHEN USING SHIELD

"One of the best things about Shield is that my friends don't know when I'm using it!" (11 year old boy.) This simple but potentially powerful tool is always available, and allows the child to be in control and to 'filter' the challenges they face.

SHIELD – THE SCRIPT

(Resources: Paper, pencil, colours)

Today we're going to do an activity that we can use when we want to feel a bit more protected. It's not meant to protect you on the outside, it's meant to help protect you on the inside; protect your thoughts and feelings. It's called Shield, and it's a bit like wrapping ourselves in a warm safe blanket that helps us to keep out the worries.

Remember what we do when we focus on success? You make sure your eyes are looking at me, you're listening very carefully, and your body is nice and still. Let's begin...

- *Can anyone tell me what a shield does?* (Share ideas to allow all the children to have a concept of a shield.)

- *Thank you. Today we're going to create an imaginary shield for ourselves that we can use whenever we need to.*

- *I want you to begin by drawing a picture of yourself on the left side of the paper.* (Let them know that the picture doesn't have to be their 'best' drawing. As long as they know what it's meant to be, that's fine.)

- *And now on the right side of the paper I'd like you to draw a worry you are facing. For example, your worry could be to do with having a different teacher, learning a new sport, making new friends or something like that.* (If this is the first time using Shield, encourage them to choose a small worry to let them focus on the technique itself.)

- *Then I'd like you to choose a colour that makes you feel protected, and colour all around the picture of you. Don't colour around the worry, though.*

- *Now comes the fun part! Close your eyes and take three nice slow Brilliant Breaths. Allow the air to go right down to your stomach before you slowly and quietly breathe out.*

- *And now as we count from one to five, I want you to see this wonderful colour surrounding your legs, your body, your arms and your head. Remember; don't worry if you find this hard to do. Just imagine what it would be like if you found it really easy to do! As I count, I want you to imagine that the lovely colour is actually surrounding your body right now. Ready?* **One, two, three, four, five.** *Fantastic! This colour is your shield!*

- *Now choose a sound that makes you feel powerful. For example, you might choose a lion roaring, children clapping, or your favourite loud music. This sound is also part of your shield. As we count from one to five, notice that this sound is all around you.* **One, two, three, four, five.** *Well done! Your shield is even stronger!*

- *Now choose a feeling that makes you feel safe and happy. This might be getting the giggles when you want to laugh, being wrapped in a duvet, or feeling the sun-shine on your face. This feeling is also part of your shield! As we count from one to five, notice that this feeling is all around you.* **One, two, three, four, five.** *Excellent! Your shield is really strong!*

- *Now do you remember that problem you were thinking of at the beginning? I'd like you to keep your eyes closed and picture that problem trying to get past your shield.*

- *Notice with a smile that it CANNOT!*

- *The colour you chose completely stops it!*

- *The sound you chose completely stops it!*

- *The feeling you chose completely stops it!*

- *The problem tries three times to get past your shield, but it just bounces off further away each time! On the third try it bounces so far away that you can hardly see the problem!*

- *Take a nice slow deep breath and realise that because the problem is no longer all around you, you feel lighter and more hopeful. This will help you to do what is necessary to feel completely differently about this problem.*

- *Finally, choose a small physical action that will immediately activate your shield, for example, gently squeezing your wrist.*

- *This shield is yours, and you can use it whenever you need to feel stronger when you face challenges. You can use it whenever you need the strength to tell a teacher or a parent about a problem, so that they can help you. Nicely done!*

WHEN SHOULD I USE IT?
Children At Home (Examples)

You might use it when your child:

- Feels too worried to be able to take action – for example, to tell an adult that he or she is being bullied
- Is anxious about going to school
- Feels worried about a particular issue – for example, if they've had an argument with a friend

Children At School (Examples)

You might use it when children:

- Are worried about an audition or a performance
- Need to feel an extra 'nudge of confidence'
- Are anxious about a change in routine

RELATED ACTIVITIES AT HOME

1. Talk with your child about the times when she or he might use Shield. (This can provide a valuable insight into the challenges your child faces.)
2. Let your child teach you how to create your own personal Shield.
3. Make links with other stories where objects provide protection – for example, Harry Potter's cloak of invisibility, the Tin Man's body in the Wizard of Oz, the shield of Saint George when he faced the dragon. How do these things help?

I JUST WONDERED...

What differences will you notice in your thoughts and actions now that you can use Shield to help you to feel differently?

SOMETHING TO CONSIDER: 'TAKE CARE' –'TAKE RISKS!'

Did you know that no-one has EVER achieved anything without taking a risk? Changing jobs, having children, moving house, playing a new game, writing a book! Risk is embedded within any change. However, 'risk-taking' is rarely acknowledged as an essential element of success. Empowering children to take risks is a key life skill. Of course, this doesn't mean risks with health or safety, but it does mean risks that reflect initiative, creativity and the inspiration to reach your goals.

TEACHING CHILDREN HOW TO:

- change their view of a future event
- recognise success
- anticipate success
- overcome setbacks
- feel inspired to take action

Seeing Success

Creating a positive outcome

"If you think you can or you think you can't – you're right!" Henry Ford

WHAT IS IT?

Seeing Success is a tool that can help to create a more positive view of a future event you are worried about.

WHY IS THIS IMPORTANT?

- There will be times when children feel anxious about a future event – for example, a new challenge, a new teacher, moving house and so on. Seeing Success is a strategy for changing a negative perspective into a more positive one.
- Fear of future failure can escalate to such a point that children worry about doing anything new.
- Seeing Success can encourage children to feel more resourceful. Even if they don't 'succeed' this time, they have strategies to enable them to see a new successful outcome.

HOW DO YOU DO IT?

Seeing Success – Summary

1. Focus on an activity or a situation that you feel unsure about – for example, meeting new people, being in a sports competition, doing a test.
2. Close your eyes and imagine you can see yourself. You are actually doing the thing you were worried about, and it is turning out really well. Turn up the colours in the picture to make it really clear (SEEING).
3. Imagine what you will say to yourself when this has gone better than you expected. Say those things to yourself right now, and make the inner voice even clearer (HEARING).
4. Imagine how you will feel when it goes much better than you thought (FEELING).
5. You have the ability to 'turn up' any of these visualisations to make them even more positive. Do so right now and enjoy the results.

REACTIONS FROM CHILDREN WHEN USING SEEING SUCCESS

Children frequently want to use this tool in relation to sporting events, auditions or tests. Rather than being inhibited by anxiety, they can train, rehearse, or revise with a clear positive outcome in mind.

SEEING SUCCESS – THE SCRIPT

Today we're going to use a tool called Seeing Success. If we are feeling worried about something that is going to take place in the future, Seeing Success can help us to feel much more positive about it. It's what outstanding achievers do all the time. Rather than focussing on 'failure', they see, hear and feel success, making these images so strong that they stay motivated day after day!

Remember what we do when we focus on success? You make sure your eyes are looking at me, you're listening very carefully, and your body is nice and still. Let's begin...

- *First of all I want you to think about what we mean by 'success'. How do you know when you are successful?* (Share some examples.)

- *Remember, success isn't just about winning trophies or being first. It's about all the successes you will have every day, when you do your best, when you overcome challenges, or when you help someone else. Think about times when you've been successful.*

- *Tell me words that communicate how you feel when you are successful.* (List these words and add any of your own.)

- *Some of these words might link with what we **see** – for example, we might see someone who is laughing, or looking confident, or who is telling friends about their success.*

- *Some of these words might link with what we **hear** – for example, 'Well done!' or 'Brilliant!' or 'Great!'*

- *Some of these words might link with what we **feel** – for example, relief, excitement, enjoyment.*

- *What Seeing Success does is to allow us to create these feelings of success and to attach them to something we might feel a bit worried about.*

- *For example, how many of you feel a bit anxious when you think about taking a test?*

- *If we were doing Seeing Success and focussing on taking a test, I might ask you to think about what you see, hear and feel just as you are about to start the test. For example, what will your face look like? Concentrating? Worried? Tired?*

- *What will you hear inside your head? For example, 'This is hard!' or 'I don't know this!*

- *What will you feel? For example, Hot? Nervous? Excited?* (Allow other children to support if required.)

- *When we use Seeing Success, we make all these things as positive as possible. Instead of seeing the test going wrong, we see it going right!*

- *Now it's your turn. Think about an activity you are going to do that you feel unsure about. For example, you might think about completing some writing, reading out loud, or playing in a team game.*

- *When you've thought of something, put your hand up.*(If only a few hands go up, share some times when most of us feel a little anxious – for example, performing in a play, meeting new people, experiencing a big change.)

- *Now I'd like you to close your eyes and imagine that you can see **yourself** in the future, and the activity you were worried about is actually happening. Do that right now. Close your eyes and imagine you are doing the activity you were worried about.*

- *But it is going really well! Much better than you expected!*

- *I want you to imagine a TV camera has moved in front of you. The camera shows that your face is smiling and you look very confident. Make it a full colour, moving picture. Focus the camera. Make your face look even happier!* ***(SEEING)***

- *Keep your eyes closed and imagine a microphone can hear the thoughts inside your head. The words are really helpful – 'I did it!' or 'That was really good!' or 'I did my best!' Say those things to yourself right now, and make the voice inside your head even clearer. **(HEARING)***

- *Keep your eyes closed and imagine how you feel now that the thing you were worried about has gone much better than you thought. You might notice that you feel calm all over. You might feel lighter in your head. You might feel excited in your stomach. Turn it up right now. Make those feelings even stronger. **(FEELING)***

- *If you find this hard to do, don't worry. Just imagine how you would feel if it was going really, really well! Enjoy that feeling now!*

- *Really notice the success you can see, hear and feel. Go on! See yourself smiling. Hear your inner voice saying 'Well done!' Feel amazing!*

- *Take a long slow deep breath right now. Fantastic! Open your eyes.*

- *Now that you've done this, I want you to experience this positive feeling whenever you think about the thing you used to be unsure about. You might even notice that the worry just doesn't seem the same anymore. You might be surprised to notice that whenever you think about this worry, you find you're not worrying! Instead, you find yourself wanting to do your best and taking action to help you do this!*

- *Let me know about times when you've been able to do this. Well done for choosing to have such a clear view of success!*

Of course, Seeing Success doesn't mean that everything will go just the way you imagine, but it does put you in a much stronger place to do whatever you need to do, and sometimes that can be all the difference that's needed.

LEAD DRIVER

'We become 'experts' at whatever we practice!' – The more we practice Seeing Success, the more inspiration we will feel and the more tenacious we will be when faced with obstacles.

WHEN SHOULD I USE IT?

Children at Home (Examples)

You might use it when your child:
- Gets butterflies in his or her stomach when thinking about something in the future
- Is worried about meeting new people
- Feels nervous about changing schools or moving house

Children at School (Examples)

You might use it when children:
- Are worried about making friends in a new school
- Are anxious about a particular curriculum subject
- Are worried about playtimes or lunchtimes

RELATED ACTIVITIES AT HOME

1. Talk with your child about times when she or he feels successful. Remember, there is a big difference between *being* successful and actually *feeling* successful!

2. Find out when your child feels 'unsuccessful'. In what ways could you help your child to feel more successful?

3. Share successes you've seen in your child – for example, getting over a 'mood', going to bed without too much fuss, bringing home a lovely piece of work, making you smile!

RELATED ACTIVITIES AT SCHOOL

1. Discuss successes the children have had. (Don't be disheartened if at first some of them can't think of any successes, or only mention doing well in tests, sports or computer games! Encourage them to recognise the many successes they will have had every day – for example, working through a headache; helping a friend; attempting a new activity and so on.)

2. Ask the children to draw a picture or create a model of a success they have had. Display these and remind them of this success when they are faced with future challenges.

3. Discuss times when they think they might need to use Seeing Success. (This can provide a very useful insight into how they view their future.)

I JUST WONDERED...

How do you know when you are 'successful'? Does someone have to tell you, or do you feel it within yourself?

SOMETHING TO CONSIDER – 'I'VE DONE IT!'

The world's greatest achievements have taken place many times in the mind of the individual long before they have occurred in reality. When preparing for the Olympics, champion competitors will be 'watching' themselves win weeks, months or even years before they are in the stadium. They will make this visualisation so focussed that they will see, hear and feel the responses of the crowds as they achieve their goal! This powerful ability to see success is critical in order to give us the tenacity to overcome the obstacles we will face along the way.

TEACHING CHILDREN HOW TO:

- understand they have a choice
- think creatively
- let go of a fear or anxiety
- share feelings with supportive peers
- let go of a label

Shrink

Letting go of barriers

"Fear defeats more people than any other one thing in the world."
Ralph Waldo Emerson, 1803–1882

WHAT IS IT?

Shrink is a way to reduce negative emotions. For example, it can help us when we feel worried, shy, or anxious but we can't really identify why. Shrink gives these feelings a tangible 'form', such as a picture or a model, and then literally shrinks them.

WHY IS THIS IMPORTANT?

- It is easy for children to feel disempowered by their emotions. Shrink can help them to feel they can have some control without having to identify what the specific issue is.
- Shrink can be particularly powerful for kinaesthetic learners because the tool requires physical responses.
- It can provide a unique insight into how children conceptualise problems –

for example, big, small, light, dark and so on – and provide an interesting catalyst for discussion.

HOW DO YOU DO IT?

Resources: A3 paper; crayons (wax crayons allow children to press lightly or hard to communicate depth of emotion)

Shrink – Summary

1. Think of something you are a bit anxious about.
2. Choose a colour that reminds you of 'anxiety' and draw the shape of this 'anxiety' on a piece of paper. *(Remember it doesn't need to be a 'picture', just a shape.)*
3. Now hold out your hands, close your eyes and picture yourself holding that anxiety shape between your hands. *(Consider size, weight, feel and so on.)*
4. On the count of ten, slowly bring your hands together and shrink the emotion.
5. Now hold what's left of the anxiety in one hand and squeeze it until it is reduced to almost nothing.
6. Hold the hand to your mouth and gently blow the last speck of the anxiety away.

REACTIONS FROM CHILDREN WHEN USING SHRINK

When using Shrink for the first time there have been many occasions when children have felt that they should draw a 'picture' of a worry. For example, they might draw the face of a child who has upset them, a picture of a dog that scared them, or a sketch of an exam paper! Emphasise that for this activity they do not need to draw a recognisable picture, simply a shape.

SHRINK – THE SCRIPT

(Resources: A3 paper, crayons)

Shrink is a fun way to let go of a worry, a fear, or an anxiety that is on our minds. It's especially useful if it's a feeling that just seems to happen to us and we have no control over it, such as 'I feel worried' or 'I feel shy'. Shrink can encourage us to take control of that feeling, make it smaller, and then 'let it go' to give us some space to feel differently.

Remember what we do when we focus on success? You make sure your eyes are looking at me, you're listening very carefully, and your body is nice and still. Let's begin...

- *What do you think is meant by the word 'anxiety'?* (Share comments.)

- *I'd like you to consider things that happen in school that children might feel a bit anxious about.* (Phrasing the question in this general way can stop children feeling personally worried. Share some of their thoughts if appropriate.)

- *Now, in order to allow you to get used to using Shrink, choose one of these anxieties to work on.*

- *The questions I'm going to ask might sound a bit unusual, so simply enjoy answering them.*

- *If the anxiety you are thinking about had a colour, what colour would it be? Don't feel anxious if you don't know! Just imagine what colour it would be if you did know!*

- *If you could hear the voice in your head, what does it say about the anxiety? For example, it might say 'I won't be any good!'*

- *If the anxiety had a feeling, what feeling would it be? For example, a knotted feeling in your stomach? A headache? A general feeling of heaviness?* (Share any examples.)

- *Now choose a crayon that is like the colour you chose for the anxiety and* *draw a **shape** on a piece of paper. **Don't** try to make it a picture. Just choose the colour and draw any shape that comes to mind. It can be big or small, smooth or jagged, in the middle of the paper or at the side, as long as it reminds you of anxiety.*

- (Once the pictures have been drawn, sharing them can be a very worthwhile experience. For example, you can share similarities, differences, thought processes and so on.)

- *Thank you.*

- *Take a final look at your shape and then put your pictures down. We need to keep our hands free for the next part.*

- *Close your eyes.*

- *Begin Brilliant Breathing. Take in nice easy breaths and allow the air to go right to your stomach before you breathe out.*

- *Keeping your eyes closed, hold out your hands. Now imagine you are actually holding the anxiety shape you have just drawn. Hold it right now. As you do this, think about how big it is, how heavy it is and what it feels like.*

- *As I count to ten, I want you to slowly bring your hands together and shrink the anxiety. Make it smaller and smaller as you hold it in your hands. As you do this, imagine you can see, hear, and feel the anxiety getting smaller and smaller. By the time I get to ten your hands will be together. Ready? **One, two, three, four, five,** it's now half the size it was, **six, seven, eight, nine, ten.** Great!*

- *Open your eyes, but keep this smaller anxiety in your hands.*

- *Now take hold of what's left of the anxiety and put it in one hand. As I count to five, squeeze your hand until the anxiety is so small it is almost nothing. Ready? **One, two, three, four, five.** Brilliant!*

- *Now carefully bring the hand to your mouth and gently blow the last speck of the anxiety away. Fantastic!*

- *Now take three brilliant breaths and really notice the difference you have chosen to make. You might notice that you feel a bit lighter, as though you have let go of a problem. Also notice that from now on when you feel a bit anxious, you can remember that you took control of anxiety and let it go! You can choose to do this again whenever you need to. Well done for choosing to explore feelings in such an imaginative way!*

WHEN SHOULD I USE IT?

Children at Home (Examples)

You might use it when your child:

- Seems to be 'weighed down' with a particular problem, but finds it hard to verbalise.
- Feels overwhelmed by a particular negative feeling – for example, feeling stressed, shy and so on.
- Seems argumentative and moody and doesn't want to talk directly about what is on their mind.

Children at School (Examples)

You might use it when children:

- Find it hard to verbalise a negative emotion.
- Need to develop a creative response to their feelings.
- Need to have the opportunity to communicate how they experience an emotion. *(Keep in mind that this representation is how they feel at **this** particular moment).*

RELATED ACTIVITIES AT HOME

1. Share times with your child when you would like to have used Shrink yourself. (Keep this 'light' but honest.)
2. You and your child each draw a Shrink shape – for example, worry, boredom, or irritation – and then compare the shapes and discuss similarities or differences.
3. A fun discussion – if Shrink was a super hero, what would he, she or it look like? What would be the super powers?

RELATED ACTIVITIES AT SCHOOL

1. Make a display of the shape-pictures the children have created. Share similarities and differences.
2. Make a clay model of a 'worry-shape' and then mould it into a positive solution.
3. Have fun doing Shrink in reverse – i.e. Expand. Change an 'ok' feeling to a 'great' feeling!

I JUST WONDERED...

Now that you can choose to literally shrink anxiety, what couldn't you do if you put your mind to it?

SOMETHING TO CONSIDER –'MIRROR NEURONS'

Neuro-science tells us that 'mirror neurons' may have intriguing implications for friendships, groups, classes of children and so on. Research suggests that when we are in the vicinity of others, we will pick up on emotions even when we are not consciously aware of them. Brain scans show areas of the brain responding in a way that 'mirrors' the strong emotions of others in the vicinity. If we can teach children to decrease negative emotions, then as well as making a difference to the individual, this might have an unforeseen positive impact on those around them.

Personal Space

Time to relax, reflect, re-energise

"The greatest revelation is stillness."   Lao-tzu

WHAT IS IT?

This is a longer script that encourages children to create a positive, safe place within themselves to support a deeper self awareness and experience a calm focussed state.

WHY IS THIS IMPORTANT?

- Personal Space encourages children to use their visual, auditory and kinaesthetic creativity to develop stillness, empathy and the ability to actually hear what is being said. (We frequently listen, but don't actually hear!)
- Personal Space can be a lovely experience to share with children as you relax together.
- Personal Space is a longer focussed imagery activity. Focussed imagery or visualisation can be an excellent teaching tool, as it allows children to

imaginatively experience things they can't directly encounter. For example, when revising a historical topic on the Romans, help them to visualise a Roman town and then ask them to describe what they can see, hear, and feel. (And smell and taste!)

HOW DO YOU DO IT?

Personal Space –Summary

1. Identify a 'relaxation number' that describes how they feel right now. Zero corresponds to very relaxed, and ten is not relaxed at all.
2. Self-massage forehead and jaw with slow circular movements.
3. Send a relaxing breath to different parts of your body.
4. Send a relaxing breath inside your head.
5. Imagine a lovely relaxing outdoor space.
6. What do you see? What do you hear? What do you feel?
7. Make all of these sensations even more vivid by adding more colours, sounds and feelings.
8. Take time to enjoy this wonderful safe relaxing place you have created. Enjoy!
9. Find out what has happened to their relaxation numbers –if they can remember them!

REACTIONS FROM CHILDREN WHEN USING PERSONAL SPACE

Children who normally find it really hard to feel calm can surprise themselves with Personal Space. Comments such as *'That was amazing!'* or *'I didn't think I could relax!'* are not uncommon. Sometimes they even fall asleep! Don't worry if this happens (*although it's probably best that **you** don't drop off!*). Sleeping shows that they were in need of a break, and once they fully wake up from this 'power-nap' it can leave them refreshed and ready to do what they need to do.

PERSONAL SPACE – THE SCRIPT

Specific Delivery Style: Lower your voice slightly. Slow, gentle, very relaxed.

Today we're going to visit a place called Personal Space. This is going to be a lovely, safe, relaxing place that you will be able to visit whenever you want to. Does that sound good?

*Before we begin I'd like you to think of a number between zero and ten that matches your level of relaxation right **now**. The lower the number, the more relaxed you are. Ten is not relaxed at all, and zero is very, very relaxed.* (They can write the numbers down if you or they wish.) *I'm going to ask you what has happened to your number when we've finished.*

Remember what we do when we focus on success? You make sure your eyes are looking at me, you're listening very carefully, and your body is nice and still. Let's begin...

- *Start by Brilliant Breathing. Take in nice easy breaths and allow the air to go all the way to your stomach before you breathe out.*

- *Place two fingers from each hand on your forehead and do slow circular movements so that you notice yourself feeling more relaxed.*

- *Slowly bring your fingers down to your cheekbones and continue these comfortable slow circular movements along your jaw.*

- *Thank you. Now relax your hands. Place them in your lap and let your shoulders relax.*

- *Now I'm sure you already know that you have an amazing skill. You can listen to my voice and make yourself become relaxed.*

- *Close your eyes and imagine that you can place 'relaxation' right in your breath. As you slowly breathe you feel more and more relaxed. Notice your breath right now.*

Allow that breath to go to your face, and notice your eyes relaxing.

Allow that breath to go to your cheeks, and notice your mouth relaxing.

Allow that breath to go to your shoulders, and notice your arms relaxing.

Allow that breath to go to your hands, and notice your fingers relaxing.

Allow that breath to go to your stomach and notice your body relaxing

Allow that breath to go all the way down to your legs, and notice your feet relaxing.

Thank you.

- *Now, notice that you can send this breath inside your head to relax your thoughts*

- *Imagine that your head feels lighter and more comfortable with each breath. Imagine the breath filling the whole of your head. Keep your eyes closed, but make this relaxation so noticeable that you smile to yourself right now. Go on, make your head so comfortable and relaxed that a smile is on your face.*

- *Don't worry if thoughts come. Simply let them go again, and focus on the lovely relaxing breath that fills your head.*

- *Now we're going to visit our Personal Space.*

- *I'd like you to keep your eyes closed and pretend that we are somewhere outdoors. It could be a garden, or somewhere quiet that you like, or somewhere you've seen in a picture. Make sure it is a lovely outdoor place, and that you feel really relaxed. Make it a lovely sunny day.*

- *With your eyes closed, imagine that you can take a look around. Look at the colour of the sky. Look at the trees or the birds. Look at all the colours you have chosen to put into your mind. Notice all the lovely calm things you can see in your personal space.*

- *Now listen to the outdoor sounds you might hear. Listen to the birds. Listen to the leaves moving as a warm wind gently blows. Listen to the quiet sound of your breathing.*

- *Now I'd like you to imagine you can feel the sun on your face. Feel the warm breeze gently blowing. Feel the soft ground underneath your feet, and notice that you feel really calm inside. You can breathe even deeper and be even more relaxed.*

- *Now I want you to realise that this is **your** personal space, so make it as lovely as you can. Add even more colours. Add even more gentle sounds. Add even more lovely feelings. Make this imagining so strong that I can tell just by looking at you that you are really relaxed.*

- *I'm going to stop talking for a little bit, but I'd like you to keep your eyes closed. I'm going to see if I can tell how relaxed you are just by looking at you. Really enjoy each breath in your lovely personal space.*

- Pause – Look for non-verbal signs of relaxation, for example, eyes closed, relaxed facial expression, gentle breathing, lowered head or body, stillness.

- *Thank you. Really breathe all of this in, and notice that your breathing is much deeper than it was.*

- *Now we're going to leave this Personal Space, but remember that it is yours and you can visit it whenever you want to breathe deeply and feel more relaxed.*

- *Take five more brilliant breaths, and when you've done this, quietly say 'well done' to yourself and then open your eyes.*

- Ask the children what has happened to their original 'relaxation number'. It will be lower than it was if they feel more relaxed, higher if they feel less relaxed. Whatever the results, the children's responses will be very useful to know.

- Don't be surprised if some of them have become so relaxed that they've forgotten the number they originally chose! Enjoy the results.

LEAD DRIVER

'The magic is in this moment' – Longer relaxation scripts can be a real eye opener for children who anticipate that stillness will be 'dull'. Understanding that there is something to experience when nothing 'active' is happening can be a unique insight for children.

WHEN SHOULD I USE IT?

Children at Home (Examples)

You might use it when your child:
- Would benefit from relaxation and you want to share a quiet peaceful time
- Has had a stressful day
- Is feeling tired but doesn't think they will be able to sleep

Children at School (Examples)

You might use it when children:
- Have finished a strenuous physical activity
- Would benefit from experiencing stillness
- Need to relax and unwind at the end of the day

RELATED ACTIVITIES AT HOME

1. Put on some quiet music and enjoy sharing the Personal Space script with your child.
2. If they're happy to do so, let your child tell you about their Personal Space.
3. Describe what you would see in your Personal Space.

RELATED ACTIVITIES AT SCHOOL

1. Ask the children if they enjoyed their Personal Space, and discuss the numbers at the beginning and the end. Did the children feel more or less relaxed?
2. What could they do to make the number even lower next time?
3. Ask the children to describe their Personal Space to a friend.

Homework! Ask the children to visit their Personal Space tonight when they go to bed and see if it helps them to have a good night's sleep.

SOMETHING TO CONSIDER – BRAINWAVES!

Have you ever forgotten something, but then later on when you are simply daydreaming or about to drop off to sleep you suddenly remember what it was? This is because you've reached the 'alpha state'. The brain uses four specific frequencies: beta, alpha, theta and delta. The beta waves (12–38 Hz on an EEG) tend to be present when we are fully alert and ready for new learning, but it is when we are experiencing the more relaxed state of alpha waves (8–12 Hz) that we are in the most receptive state to recall information. (Useful to know when revising!)

In addition to this, a research project led by Chris Berka at Advanced Brain Monitoring in Carlsbad, California suggests that the alpha state is linked with excellence. The research group found that the alpha waves in the brain patterns of professional golfers and Olympic archers increased just as they were about to compete. This was always more evident in experts than in novices. The researchers stated that '*this represents focussed attention on the target while other sensory inputs are suppressed*'. The change in brainwaves was accompanied by a slower breathing rate and a lower pulse rate. Activities such as listening to calm music, Brilliant Breathing or experiencing relaxing visualisations can help us to reach the alpha state.

TEACHING CHILDREN HOW TO:

- recognise their own qualities and successes
- feel they can change if they wish to do so
- develop resilience and tenacity
- recognise the qualities and successes of others
- develop the impact of the Jacket with use

The Jacket

Developing resilience; recognising strengths

"People are beginning to realize that success takes more than intellectual excellence or technical prowess, and that we need another sort of skill to survive – and certainly to thrive – in the increasingly turbulent job market of the future. Internal qualities such as resilience, initiative, optimism, and adaptability are taking on a new valuation."
Daniel Goleman – Working with Emotional Intelligence

WHAT IS IT?

The Jacket is a way to remind ourselves of the qualities we have within ourselves that can enable us to overcome the challenges we face. It can help us to develop tenacity, resilience and optimism.

WHY IS THIS IMPORTANT?

- The Jacket can be used to help children to overcome setbacks, to develop the resilience to respond effectively to peers who don't treat them well or situations that are challenging.

- The Jacket can be a prompt to help children to remember their successes.
- A reminder of all the things they have already managed to achieve, which will then support them with the current problem.
- The Jacket can be used by a child at any time. One simple movement, such as 'zipping up the front', can provide an anchor into a more resourceful state.

HOW DO YOU DO IT?
(Resources: Paper, pencil, colours)

The Jacket – Summary

1. Imagine you have a very special jacket.
2. Draw this jacket on a large piece of paper, and on the front of it write or draw lots of things that you have done well.
3. Close your eyes and imagine putting the jacket on. Notice that as soon as you put it on you find yourself feeling much more positive.
4. You see, hear and feel much more confident as you recognise all the inner resources you possess that will help you to exceed expectations.
5. You remember your skills and successes and feel more able to get over obstacles to reach your goal.

REACTIONS FROM CHILDREN WHEN USING THE JACKET

Don't be surprised if you see some children 'doing up the zips' on their jackets at times you might not expect, for example, before a party; before break-times; before a school trip. This can provide important information about the challenges they expect to face.

THE JACKET – THE SCRIPT

(Resources: Paper, pencil, colours)

This tool is called The Jacket, and we can use it to help us to feel a bit stronger if we are worried about something. I don't mean stronger in our hands or arms, but stronger in our minds. Today we will use it to help us to feel stronger if we face a problem to do with change. This change could be moving to a new class or school, moving house, making new friends and so on.
For this example we will focus on the challenge of making new friends.

Remember what we do when we focus on success? You make sure your eyes are looking at me, you're listening very carefully, and your body is nice and still. Let's begin...

- *I'd like you to imagine that you are just about to go into a room where there are three different groups of children playing board games. The children are all about your age, but you don't know any of them.*

- *Who would feel excited about meeting them?* (Share responses.)

- *Who might feel a bit nervous?* (Share responses.) *Well, this tool can help to give us that extra bit of confidence, however we feel.*

- *I want you to think of a jacket. It can be a style of your choice, but make sure it has a large zip that does up the front. Have you thought of one?*

- *This is a very special jacket because it can make you feel stronger and more able to deal with problems.*

- *I'd like you to use a pencil, not colours yet, to draw this jacket on your piece of paper. Make it big. Use the whole of the piece of paper so that you will have space to draw things on the jacket itself. Remember to draw the zip at the front of the jacket. Off you go.*

- *Now I'd like you to write or draw and colour your successes on the jacket. You can put any things that **you** have done well, any skills you have, and* *things that help you to remember your achievements. For example, you might draw a picture of you getting a high score on a computer game, or you helping another child, or you writing a great story, or you riding a bike. Choose things that you're really pleased with, that make you think, 'Yes. I did well!' Remember – your successes don't have to be like anybody else's, as long as they are important to you!* (Give them time to do this. Share supportive ideas and celebrate successes.) *Well done.*

- NB: Make a note of any child who finds this particularly challenging. He or she would probably benefit from doing My Choice of Inner Voice, Seeing Success or Enjoying Excellence.

- Ask children to share some of their successes and encourage everyone to applaud or cheer!

- *Thank you very much! The stronger we can make the good feelings linked with this jacket, the more support it can give us.*

- *Take one last look at your picture and smile as you think about the brilliant successes you have had.*

- *Now I'd like you to close your eyes.*

- *I want you to imagine putting on the jacket you have drawn – the one with the zip at the front and all the successes you have placed on it. This special jacket holds all those successes, all those things you have done well and that are special about you. Put it on right now, but don't zip up the front yet.*

- *Good. I'm going to count from one to five, and as I count I want you to slowly zip up the jacket. As you hear each number I want you to really notice all those successes that you have had. Notice that they are part of the jacket and, most importantly, part of you.*

- *Ready? You are about to zip up the front of this very special jacket. Keep your eyes closed, and as you do up the zip concentrate on your successes. Here we go.* **One, two, three, four, five.** *Fantastic!*

- *Keep your eyes closed and notice that as soon as you zip the jacket up, you find yourself feeling stronger! It sounds incredible, but notice that you can actually choose to feel more confident now that you are wearing this amazing jacket. Make this feeling as powerful as you can right now!*

- *By the way, this jacket with all your successes is completely invisible to everyone else, but you can feel the fantastic effect it has on your confidence!*

- *Remember at the start I talked about making new friends? Imagine you are walking into that room I mentioned, where there are three groups of children playing board games. You still don't know any of them, but as you walk in through the door you imagine zipping up the front of your incredible invisible jacket! You instantly choose to feel more confident!*

- *Keep your eyes closed, but imagine you can see yourself looking at the three groups of children who are playing board games. You go over to the first group and ask to join in. They say no! But because you feel stronger than you did before, you go over to the second group and ask to join in. They say they don't need any more players. But because you feel stronger than you did before, you walk over to the third group and ask to join in. They let you play!*

- *Imagine you can **see** yourself laughing with your new friends.*

- *Imagine you can **hear** the voice inside your head saying 'This is fun!'*

- *Imagine you are wearing your jacket and you **feel** really pleased that you didn't give up when the other children said 'no', because now you've made some new friends!*

- *From now on you can put this special jacket on whenever you want to feel stronger inside yourself. It is your jacket, and the more you wear it the more you can choose to notice the successes you have had and the skills you possess. This awareness can help to give you the confidence to get past the challenges that come your way.*

LEAD DRIVER

'Rapport with others is very important. Rapport with ourselves is essential' – Recognising the qualities of others and the many qualities we possess can help us to feel success is within our reach.

WHEN SHOULD I USE IT?

Children at Home (Examples)

You might use it when your child:
- Would benefit from feeling more resilient after setbacks

- Has to cope with 'losing' and needs to develop the tenacity to move on
- Finds it hard to remember how successful he or she is

Children at School (Examples)

You might use it when children:

- Need to develop resilience when faced with setbacks
- Would benefit from recognising and sharing strengths
- Need to feel empowered after a negative experience

RELATED ACTIVITIES AT HOME

1. Discuss times when your child might use The Jacket.
2. Share the many successes your child has had, or the qualities he or she possesses, that could be written on the jacket. For example, you might talk about playing games with you, getting over being 'fed up', helping a sibling, riding a bike, making you feel happy and so on.
3. Put on a jacket from your wardrobe. Imagine it is a 'special one' and have fun reminding your child about some of *your* qualities! *(Hopefully they will recognise some of them!)*

RELATED ACTIVITIES AT SCHOOL

1. Share the jacket drawings and then ask the children to imagine putting on their jackets. They can share their qualities with a friend. *(For children who find this difficult, ask the friend to identify some of their qualities.)*
2. Ask the children to write a story called 'The child who found a very special jacket!'
3. Display the drawings of the jackets and let the children add to their successes over time – for example, when they successfully use other tools to overcome challenges.

SOMETHING TO CONSIDER – ANCHORS

Practitioners of Neuro-Linguistic Programming frequently refer to 'anchors'. These are learned patterns of response that link to specific stimuli. For example, the phone rings and we feel the need to answer it, the teacher asks a question and children put their hands up (mostly!), the bell goes and playtime ends. Research and practice in NLP has discovered that we can create anchors that support us. These are response patterns that make us feel more positive.

The Jacket is such an anchor. The 'trigger' is pulling up the imaginary zip at the front of the imaginary jacket. This can immediately anchor us into a more resourceful state if we vividly recall the qualities and successes embedded into the jacket. The more positive the feelings linked to the anchor; the stronger the support.

THE PHASE THREE TOOLS

1. Change Your Mind
2. Step Forward
3. Enjoying Excellence
4. Fab Future
5. Eye of the Storm

PHASE THREE GOALS

For children:

a. to frequently make empowering choices that support their success

b. to use the tools proficiently, creatively and independently, adjusting them to match their particular needs

c. to have the skill, sensitivity and insight to advise others on how to experience success

d. to regularly **be** and **feel** successful

e. to be able to critically assess their own progress, and to skilfully act upon outcomes

TEACHING CHILDREN HOW TO:

- realise they have a choice
- notice the way they visualise a problem
- focus on resolution
- identify the solution to a problem
- be pro-active

Change Your Mind

Seeing a solution rather than a problem.

"Habits of thinking need not be forever. One of the most significant findings in psychology in the last twenty years is that individuals can choose the way they think."
Martin Seligman – Learned Optimism

WHAT IS IT?

Change Your Mind can help children to envisage a positive outcome. When children think of a problem they often give it certain visual qualities in their minds. These scenes can sometimes be quite negative and emotionally draining. These inner pictures will of course vary from child to child, but when they carry strong emotions, the images inside their heads are sometimes large, full colour, centred and moving. Change Your Mind allows a child to alter how their mind 'sees' a problem and to learn how to picture a solution.

WHY IS THIS IMPORTANT?

- Change Your Mind allows children to have a practical way to change their perspective concerning a problem. *(It is particularly powerful for children who enjoy visual imagery.)*

- Change Your Mind allows children to begin to think about how they view a challenge inside their heads.
- It encourages children to consider the first step to solving a problem and feeling more successful.
- The new solution-focussed pictures can be a tangible reminder of a goal.

HOW DO YOU DO IT?

(Resources: Large piece of paper, pencil, wax crayons and a display of the instructions set out in steps 2 and 4 below.)

Change Your Mind – Summary

1. Identify the problem that's on your mind, and think of an image or picture that clearly reminds you of this.
2. Draw this image, but follow these instructions: a) use a pencil; b) press lightly; c) draw the image slightly to the side of the paper; d) make it small.
3. Now identify an image that would mean that you have *solved the problem*.
4. Draw this image, but follow these instructions. Draw it *on the same paper so it completely covers the small one,* and a) use pencil and colours; b) press quite hard; c) place it in the centre of the paper; d) make it BIG! *(However, leave a space at the bottom to write one sentence.)*
5. Now imagine this is a moving image. Would it be rolling, flashing, spinning or something else?
6. When you look at the image, notice how you feel now that you see a much stronger solution to the problem.
7. Close your eyes and picture this big bright new moving image that shows a solution to your problem. See it, hear it, feel it.
8. At the bottom of the paper, write down the first thing you are going to do to help you get to this more positive image.

REACTIONS FROM CHLDREN WHEN USING CHANGE YOUR MIND

It may seem strange, but some children don't like drawing over the original picture of their worry! This may relate to an attachment to the worry itself. For many complex reasons it can sometimes be hard for a child to 'let go' of a worry. For example, having a problem might be a way to get the attention they want, or if a problem is resolved too quickly or too easily, it might appear to invalidate the worry itself. Of course, it could simply be that the child doesn't want to cover up the careful drawing they've just done!

CHANGE YOUR MIND – THE SCRIPT

Resources: Large piece of paper, pencil, wax crayons and a display of the instructions. For the 'problem image', follow these instructions: a) use a pencil; b) press lightly; c) draw the image slightly to the side of the paper; d) make it small.

For the 'solution image', follow these instructions. Draw it *on the same paper so it completely covers the small one* but also: a) use pencil and colours; b) press quite hard; c) place it in the centre of the paper; d) make it BIG! (However, leave a space at the bottom to write one sentence.)

Today we're going to use a tool called Change Your Mind. This tool isn't just about changing what you say, but actually changing how you think about a problem.

Remember what we do when we focus on success? You make sure your eyes are looking at me, you're listening very carefully, and your body is nice and still. Let's begin...

- *I'd like you all to sit up straight and close your eyes.*
- *Begin Brilliant Breathing. Take in nice easy breaths and allow the air to go right to your stomach before you breathe out.*
- *As you breathe, relax your jaw.*
- *As you breathe, relax your shoulders.*
- *I'd like you to think of a worry that's on your mind. It doesn't need to be a big one, because this is a new activity – just something that makes you feel a bit unsure. For example, it may be disagreeing with a friend, being a bit late for school, or not doing quite as well as you hoped in a sport.*
- *Now I'd like you to choose an image or a picture that clearly reminds you of this worry. When you've done this, open your eyes.*

- *On the piece of paper in front of you I'd like you to draw this image, but before you do, listen to these instructions.*

- **Only use a pencil. This is a black and white image.** (You are getting the children to decrease the emphasis of the problem.)

- **Press lightly with the pencil.** (Taking away depth, and encouraging the children to make the problem 'lighter'.)

- **Draw the image slightly to the side of the paper, not quite in the middle.** (Moving the problem aside.)

- **Make the image small – no bigger than the length of your little finger.** (Encouraging the children to give it some distance)

- *Off you go. (*Give whatever encouragement or support is required.)

- *Thank you. Now, take a look at the image and notice whether you feel a bit differently about the problem now that you're seeing it in this way.* (Share thoughts about making a problem less obvious, further away from you, 'lighter' and so on, but don't worry if at this stage they haven't noticed any changes about how they feel.)

- *Now I want you to close your eyes and think of an image that would mean that you have solved the problem.* (Ask them to open their eyes. Give support and share some ideas.)

- *I want you to draw this image* **on the same paper so that it completely covers the small image,** *and this time:*

- **Use pencil AND colours.**

- **Press quite hard.**

- **Place your image in the centre of the paper.**

- **Make it BIG! (But leave a space at the bottom to write one sentence.)**

- **Make sure the new 'solution' is so big that it covers the small 'problem'.**

- *Off you go!* (Repeat instructions as necessary.)

- *Thank you. Now I'd like you to look at this new picture, and imagine it is a* **moving image.** *For example, it might be rolling, shining; flashing; spinning and so on.*

- *This is the fun part. Close your eyes and picture your big bright positive moving image. Picture it right now.*

- *Add even more movement to this incredible image! Twirling? Spiralling? Twisting?*

- *Add wonderful sounds to this incredible image! Sizzling? Whirring? Zooming?*

- *Add fantastic feelings to this incredible image! Exciting? Inspiring? Amazing?*

- *Be as creative as you can! Make sure you make this image really bright and brilliant and amazing! I'll be able to tell you're doing this just by looking at you.*

- *Open your eyes. Wow! Well done! You clearly put a lot of thought into learning how to see a solution rather than a problem.*

- Now talk with the child about possible actions they might take to solve their problem, or if using the technique with a class, ask them to work in pairs to identify the first step towards their solution.

- *At the bottom of the paper, write down the first thing you are going to do to help you get to this fantastic solution!*

LEAD DRIVER

'We are learning all day every day' Realising that we can learn to see a solution rather than a problem, can have a massive impact on our daily expectations of success.

WHEN SHOULD I USE IT?

Children at Home (Examples)

You might use it when your child:

- Can't stop focussing on a problem
- Can't think of a way to resolve a problem
- Would benefit from talking about a problem and working with you to consider a way forward

Children at School (Examples)

You might use it when children:

- Need to learn that problems have a range of possible responses
- Need to be solution-focussed when dealing with challenges

- Are very visual and would benefit from exploring how they 'see' images inside their heads

RELATED ACTIVITIES AT HOME

1. Use Change Your Mind with your child and discuss pictures, thoughts and feelings.
2. Share a time when you have 'got over' a challenge.
3. Discuss the importance of the 'first step' when dealing with a challenge.

RELATED ACTIVITIES AT SCHOOL

1. Make a display of the solution focussed pictures the children have drawn.
2. Have the class share their 'first steps' and consider how they could help each other to take these steps.
3. Do Change Your Mind on a large sheet of paper in a whole school assembly.

I JUST WONDERED...

Does having a problem mean we automatically have to feel 'fed up'?

SOMETHING TO CONSIDER – 'NEUROPLASTICITY'

Our thoughts change our brains! Neurocience has discovered that our brains are much more flexible than we ever suspected. This is referred to as 'neuroplasticity'. The ability of the brain to **literally** change as a result of new thoughts and experiences. This has major implications for all of us, as it means that the ability to learn, grow and adapt is always within us. *"The discovery of neuroplasticity, that our thoughts can change the structure and function of our brains, even into old age, is the most important breakthrough in our understanding of the brain in four hundred years."* Norman Doidge PhD

The question is, do our daily thoughts help us to develop supportive neural pathways in the brain, or do they create beliefs and response patterns that limit our success?

TEACHING CHILDREN HOW TO:

- feel more connected to a goal
- have fun 'experiencing' the future
- develop greater motivation
- create a more positive future for themselves
- help others to aspire

Step Forward

Moving towards a powerful goal

"This is a compelling future. In fact, it is so compelling it already exists here and now in their minds and in their feelings."
Ian McDermott & Wendy Jago *The NLP Coach*

WHAT IS IT?

Step Forward is a tool that can inspire children to reach an important goal.

WHY IS THIS IMPORTANT?

- Step Forward can be a powerful tool for raising levels of aspiration.
- Step Forward can provide a unique insight into how children view goals, especially if the goals have been 'given' to them. Do they care if they reach these goals? Do they understand the difference these goals will actually make? Are they worthwhile goals?
- Step Forward can help children to connect to a goal.

HOW DO YOU DO IT?

Step Forward – Summary

Resources: Five labelled cards with the following sentences:

1. I can see...
2. I feel...
3. My inner voice is saying...
4. I've learnt that I am...
5. The new skill I now have is...

Step Forward can be very effective with one child who has a specific goal. (If other children are present they can observe and give support. Alternatively, if you make enough cards children can work in pairs.)

1. Ask a child to think about their goal. This should be something they really want to do.
2. Ask the child to close his or her eyes and imagine they have just reached their goal.
3. Applaud the goal.
4. Now ask the child to step onto each of the five cards and finish the sentences, saying what is different now that they've just reached their goal.
5. Everyone share supportive comments.
6. Give the child time to enjoy experiencing the goal. Then get them to consider the following question: What's the first step I can take to make this goal actually happen? (Again, share supportive ideas.)

REACTIONS FROM CHILDREN WHEN USING STEP FORWARD

Sometimes children will move from card to card and find it very difficult to finish the sentences. This might be due to language skills or confidence, but it is also worth considering that the goal itself doesn't really inspire them and it might need rethinking.

STEP FORWARD – THE SCRIPT

(Resources: Five step forward cards)

Script for using the tool with one child. (If sharing this tool with a class, the rest of the children can be the supportive audience. Alternatively, if you prefer and if you have enough cards, they can work in groups or pairs.)

Today we're going to use a tool called Step Forward. This tool can help us to feel more in touch with a target or a goal that we have.

Remember what we do when we focus on success? You make sure your eyes are looking at me, you're listening very carefully, and your body is nice and still. Let's begin...

- *Now, to show you how to use this tool I need someone who has a special goal they hope to reach. This will be something that you hope to achieve that will make you feel really good when you've done it.*

- *Who has a goal they will be excited to reach?*

- (If using this with a class for the first time, choose a child who has a clear goal – for example, to learn to swim twenty-five metres – and who is confident enough to share her or his thoughts.

- Ask the child to come out to the front, making sure you have enough space to lay down the five Step Forward cards.)

- *Thank you for coming out and helping me. Would you remind me again what your goal is?*

- *Lovely. Now I'd like you to close your eyes and imagine you have **just** reached that goal! Really imagine what that's like. Imagine how you feel now that you've finally done it!* (If you are doing this with a class, at this point you can ask the other children to watch carefully to see if they can see a difference in body language; facial expression and so on when the goal is 'reached'.) *You can open your eyes now. Well done for choosing to imagine you've reached your goal. I think you deserve a round of applause!*

- *Now that you're really imagining that you've just reached your goal, I'd like you to step onto each of the five cards I'm going to put down here on the floor, and finish the sentences written on them. Say your sentences in a lovely loud voice. Make sure you're imagining that you have just **this minute finally reached your goal**!*

- *I want to know what you can see, hear, feel and what you have found out about yourself.* (If required, feel free to give any prompts or support as the child steps onto each card. For example, for a goal to swim twenty-five metres the responses could be: **I can see** my friends cheering; **I feel** tired but fantastic; **My inner voice is saying** I did it; **I've learnt that I am** a good swimmer; **The new skill I now have is** being able to swim twenty-five metres.

  1. **I can see...**

  2. **I feel...**

  3. **My inner voice is saying...**

  4. **I've learnt that I am...**

  5. **The new skill I now have is...**

- *Thank you very much for sharing your goal.* (Share any **supportive** comments or insights.)

- *You've done really well! Thanks very much for volunteering! This definitely deserves another round of applause!*

- Have the child return to his or her seat.

- After the child has had a chance to enjoy the experience, share ideas about a positive step that can be taken to help to make this goal a reality.

LEAD DRIVER

'All decisions need action' – Whatever our goal, it can only become a reality by taking the first step.

WHEN SHOULD I USE IT?

Children at Home (Examples)

You might use it when your child:
- Is thinking about a goal they would like to achieve

- Has an exciting goal to share
- Appears disinterested in a goal and you want to understand his or her thoughts about it

Children at School (Examples)

You might use it when children:
- Need to seriously consider a goal
- Have a target or goal and you want to know their thoughts
- Need an opportunity to be supportive of each other's aspirations

---

RELATED ACTIVITIES AT HOME

1. Discuss your child's aspirations. If they cannot think of any goals, simply share a range of possibilities without directing them to any specific one – for example, to read longer books from the library, to be able to play chess, to be really good at a computer game, or to be in the school sports team.

2. If your child has a particular goal, consider what steps might need to be taken for them to reach this goal. How could you support them?

3. Try not to immediately judge a goal if it appears to be unrealistic. For example, their goal might be to become 'a famous celebrity'. Discuss what they think this will bring them. This can be a real insight. You can also break most goals down into important generic skills – for example, the ability overcome challenges, the ability to learn from criticism, the ability to take action and so on.

RELATED ACTIVITIES AT SCHOOL

1. Make a display of goals and first steps that the children have identified.

2. Discuss how the children felt as they walked from one card to the next. What action will they take if they do, or do not, reach their goal?

3. Identify other tools that could help children to take the first step toward achieving their goal.

I JUST WONDERED...

What will have to happen
for you to know that you've
finally reached your goal?

SOMETHING TO CONSIDER – GETTING UNDERNEATH THE SURFACE

Robert Dilts identified neurological levels (*Dynamic Learning,* Dilts and Epstein 1995), which can help us to examine personal development; relationships; roles and so on.

For example in relation to careers...

vision - whether our role supports our sense of purpose;

identity, whether our role supports our sense of self;

beliefs, whether our role is in alignment with our beliefs/values;

capability, whether our role matches and extends the skills we possess;

behaviour, whether the actions we take reflect our role;

environment, whether our surroundings support or hinder our role.

This structure can provide a powerful insight into what is actually going on beneath the surface of an organisation, a goal, an experience and so on.

TEACHING CHILDREN HOW TO:

- understand what is meant by excellence
- recognise the qualities they have that can help them to achieve excellence
- understand that excellence is linked with choice and action
- understand that excellence is linked with a feeling
- exceed their own expectations

Enjoying Excellence

Exceeding expectations

"Learning is the greatest game in life and most fun. All children are born believing this and will continue to believe this until we convince them that learning is very hard work and unpleasant. Some children never really learn this lesson, and go through life believing that learning is fun and the only game worth playing. We have a name for such people. We call them geniuses."
G. Doman – The Institute for the Achievement of Human Potential, Philadelphia, USA

WHAT IS IT?

The Oxford English Dictionary defines excellence as *"a talent or quality which is unusually good and so surpasses ordinary standards."* Enjoying Excellence is a way to encourage children to surpass ordinary standards and exceed expectations. It focuses on excellence, (in all its forms), and encourages children to let go of any limiting self beliefs that imply that excellence is beyond them. Enjoying Excellence can help to motivate children to take steps towards reaching their potential.

WHY IS THIS IMPORTANT?

- Helping children to feel more familiar with excellence will give them a clearer understanding of what it means to exceed ordinary standards.
- It's important for children to view excellence not just as an award, a grade or a certificate, but as a way of being.
- If children can appreciate excellence within themselves, then it will help to balance times when they feel overly critical of themselves.

HOW DO YOU DO IT?

'Enjoying Excellence' – Summary (Resources: pencil, paper, colours)

1. Consider the possibility that 'excellence' is not something outside of us, but within us. (If it is within us, there is **always** the possibility of accessing excellence.)
2. Explore the wider meaning of 'excellence'.
3. Recognise the innate skills and qualities we all possess that place excellence within our reach. For example, we all have curiosity; the drive to overcome problems; the ability to learn and so on.
4. Draw a matchstick figure and label it with actions that link with excellence – for example, helping someone, working out a problem, doing really well in a game.
5. Choose one of these labels, or create a new one that reflects a quality, skill or action that reflects *your* ability to achieve excellence.
6. See, hear, feel and enjoy a powerful feeling of excellence.
7. Close your eyes and visualise this strong image of excellence being inside you.
8. What is the first step you will take to achieve excellence?

REACTIONS FROM CHILDREN WHEN USING ENJOYING EXCELLENCE

When using this tool, some children have found it very challenging to consider that they could ever be excellent! If you find a child lacks confidence in this way, the discussion about the inner qualities that can lead to excellence, (qualities we all possess), takes on even greater importance. It may also be worth encouraging the child to use other confidence building tools such Personal Power; My Choice of Inner Voice and The Jacket.

'ENJOYING EXCELLENCE' – THE SCRIPT

(Resources: paper, pencil, colours)

Begin with a general discussion about 'excellence'. What does it mean? How do you know when you achieve it? Can everyone achieve it given the right circumstances? Encourage the children to challenge limitations around the concept of excellence – for example, 'I could never...' or 'You have to be in the top group...' and so on.

Remember what we do when we focus on success? Make sure your eyes are looking at me, you're listening very carefully and your body is nice and still. Let's begin...

- *Enjoy Brilliant Breathing. Take in nice easy breaths and allow the air to go right to your stomach before you breathe out.*

- *I'd like you to consider the possibility that 'excellence' is not something outside of us, but is inside us. Can you do that? (If they can't, then respond with, I understand, but imagine you **can** do this and notice the difference.)*

- *This might help. Do you know that we are born with qualities that can allow us to be excellent? These are qualities such as curiosity, the drive to overcome problems, and the ability to learn.*

- *Think of a very young child who picks up a toy hammer. This is curiosity. She tries to hold it and hit a toy peg, but she misses. As time goes by she keeps on trying until she succeeds. This is the drive to overcome problems. The next time she picks up the hammer she knows immediately how to hold it and how to bang the peg. This is the ability to learn.*

- *Put your hand up if you have ever wanted to find something out. (Share examples of curiosity if appropriate.)*

- *Put your hand up if you have ever thought something was going to be much too hard, but then you managed to do it anyway. (Share examples of the drive to overcome problems and our ability to learn. if appropriate.)*

- *We are born with the skills and qualities that can help us to be excellent. They are inside of us. Do you realise that this means they cannot actually go anywhere? The possibility of excellence is always with us.*

- *But remember, there are many ways to show excellence. It's not just about top marks, trophies and certificates. It can include the way we deal with setbacks, the way we help another child, the way we do our best and so on.*

- *I'd like you to draw a picture of a person. Just a matchstick person will be fine.*

- *Now label your figure with actions that you think are linked with excellence. For example, you might use labels such as being very kind to someone, solving a tricky problem, doing really well in a game and so on. (Share ideas and give as much support as required.)*

- *Now put a circle around the action that you feel most strongly about. If you need to add an extra one to the picture, do that now and then circle it. Make sure it gives you a clear picture of excellence and it's something you feel strongly about.*

- *Now I'd like you to close your eyes and take three nice slow deep breaths.*

- *Imagine you can see this image of excellence. You can see the action you circled, and you are doing it right now! You are achieving excellence!*

- *Notice how excellence feels. You can really enjoy it!*

- *Notice what it is like to feel excellence inside yourself. Make this as imaginative and enjoyable as you can.*

- *I want to see how you sit when you are feeling excellence.*

- *Even though your eyes are closed, I want to be able to tell you are thinking of excellence just by looking at your face.*

- *Now take another look at excellence. Do you understand that it is closer than you thought? The possibility of excellence is always inside you. You always have a choice about whether you take the action needed to uncover excellence.*

- *Take in three brilliant breaths and breathe in this excellence that is a part of you. Well done!*

- *Now I'd like you to open your eyes and consider these questions.*

- *How will you know when you show excellence while you are doing your work? What will teachers notice?*

- *How will you know when you show excellence at home? What will adults notice?*

- *How will you know when you show excellence when playing a game? What will friends notice?*

- *How will you know when you show excellence in the action you take? What will you notice?* (Give the children enough time to reflect on these questions individually, or as part of a discussion.)

- *Thank you. I'd just like you to close your eyes for one last time.*

- *Now that you know that excellence is always within you, you might surprise yourself when you find you are doing your very best. You might find that you keep going with things when previously you would have given up. You might find that you look back on your day and you feel great, because once again you have shown yourself that you can achieve excellence!*

- *Take a moment to reflect and enjoy this new understanding.* (Give them as much time as you consider appropriate.)

- *Just before you open your eyes I want you to consider this. What first step can you take that will prove to you that excellence is inside of you? Thank you.*

LEAD DRIVER

'Flexibility opens opportunities'– By being flexible and adopting a new attitude towards excellence, we can understand that excellence is always a possibility, if we choose to take the appropriate action.

WHEN SHOULD I USE IT?

Children at Home (Examples)

You might use it when your child:

- Is very motivated and wants to do well
- Has shown excellence and you want to have the opportunity to appreciate and 'share' this achievement
- Believes they could never be excellent at anything

Children at School (Examples)

You might use it when children:

- Need to understand that they have the inner resources to achieve excellence
- Have shown excellence and you want to them to recognise what they have achieved
- Would benefit from understanding that excellence is linked with a feeling

---

RELATED ACTIVITIES AT HOME

1. Talk with your child about what they think is meant by the word excellence.
2. Talk about different types of behaviour that can link with excellence – for example, doing our very best, helping others, learning from our mistakes and so on.
3. Share times when you've witnessed your child excel.

If your child finds it hard to believe that excellence is within him or herself, don't worry. Most of us find this a challenge! You can support by identifying times when he or she has shown excellence – for example, making you feel truly happy, helping a sibling, doing well at school and so on.

RELATED ACTIVITIES AT SCHOOL

1. Discuss the difference between 'good' and 'excellent'. Include the 'non-measurable' – for example, kindness – as well as the measurable – for example, a maths test result.
2. Discuss the children's concepts of excellence. If they find it hard to go beyond awards, praise, trophies and so on, then consider broader forms of excellence. For example, they might consider excellent attitudes; excellent friendships; excellent ways of behaving and so on.
3. Talk about goals and aspirations. How will they know when they have achieved excellence?

Success in Schools

SOMETHING TO CONSIDER – THE POWER TO DELETE!

Human beings have an amazing ability. We can 'delete' almost anything so that it passes beyond our conscious awareness. We can stop hearing cars when living near a busy road; we don't see the pen when we are looking for a pencil; when we walk into a room we delete the colour of the carpet until someone brings it to our attention. We need this ability to filter information; otherwise we would be overloaded by our senses. Unfortunately this can also mean we delete things we should be aware of, like the voice of a parent or teacher, the homework we 'forget', or the inner resources that can compel us towards excellence! The tools in this book remind us of personal qualities we need to be aware of!

TEACHING CHILDREN HOW TO:

- develop aspirations
- consider a more positive perspective
- feel they can influence their outcomes
- question limits they have set themselves or others have 'given' to them
- identify specific steps to success

Fab Future

Consciously placing supportive goals into our future

"Envisioning the end is enough to put the means in motion."
Dorothea Brande

WHAT IS IT?

Fab Future is a tool that can help children to 'create' a more positive future, which can be a powerful catalyst for making it a reality.

WHY IS THIS IMPORTANT?

- Fab Future can help children to aspire to long-term success and take action to achieve it.
- It can encourage children to aim for the excellent or the inspirational rather than just settling for the safe option if it does not match their potential.
- This activity can stimulate wonderful creativity as children relate their 'experiences' of 'travelling' and the 'sights' they see.
- Future worries or 'shadows' can be replaced with new positive images.

HOW DO YOU DO IT?
(Resources: Paper and pencil)

Fab Future – Summary

1. Decide on something specific that you want to achieve in the future.
2. Make this goal as vivid as you can and draw a picture of it.
3. Now imagine this powerful goal melts into your hands.
4. Close your eyes and picture a long wide path to your 'future' stretching out in front of you.
5. You begin to travel safely and happily into your fab future.
6. When you reach the right time where you want to place the goal, pour it from your hands onto the path.
7. See, hear and feel it becoming part of your new future.
8. Notice and enjoy the changes you have made.

NB: Remember that the focus is only on creating positive future events – for example, ones that support ourselves or others.

REACTIONS FROM CHILDREN WHEN USING FAB FUTURE

Have fun with this. It can be a wonderful activity to observe. The children's descriptions of their 'path into the future' and the experience of 'travelling' can be very inspirational. Watch the expressions of children when they have got their eyes closed but they're speeding along their path. You will see some who physically 'move', and others who are completely still but who reveal so much in their facial expressions.

FAB FUTURE – THE SCRIPT

(Resources: Paper, pencil.)

We're going to have fun doing something a little different today. Does anyone like the idea of making the future even better? We're going to do something called Fab Future, which is a way that can help us to change how we feel about something that is going to happen one day. It could be tomorrow, next week, next month or even next year!

I'll show you what I mean. This is just an example. Let's imagine it's the end of the school year, and you are moving to a new class. For many of you this will be an exciting time that you will look forward to, but for some of you the thought of the change might make you feel a bit nervous. Let's do Fab Future to help everyone to feel as good as they can about this change.

Remember what we do when we focus on success? You make sure your eyes are looking at me, you're listening very carefully, and your body is nice and still. Let's begin...

- *First we need to agree what we're a little concerned about. For this example, we're imagining we're unsure about moving classes at the end of the year.*

- *Now I want you to think about how you will know when the future worry has gone. This might be you walking into the new class and the teacher smiles at you. It might be as you meet new friends. It might when you are telling someone at home about the good day you've had.*

- *For this example, let's choose 'you are telling someone at home about the good day you've had'.*

- *First of all I want you to draw a picture that shows you telling someone at home about your really good day in your new class. Enjoy doing this. Drawing the picture can help you to really know this image.*

- *Thank you. Now pick up your picture and take a good look at it. Remember that this picture shows you telling someone about the good day you had in your new class.*

- *Now this might seem unusual, but I'd like you to place your hands on your picture and use your brilliant imagination. That's right. Place both your hands on your picture.*

- *Now I want you to close your eyes. Ready? Take five slow deep breaths, and imagine that the picture actually goes into your hands! That's right! It smoothly and silently goes into your hands, and now you are holding your bright new future! There might be colours slipping onto your fingers, or feelings sliding up your hands! Imagine this so strongly that you actually notice your fingers feel tingly, or warmer, or cooler! As always, don't worry if you find this hard to do – just choose to feel how you would feel if it was incredibly easy to do! When you've done this, open your eyes.*

- *Now you've got this bright new picture in your hands, it's time to make the change!*

- *I want you to imagine a path stretching out in front of you for an incredibly long way. This path goes all the way into your future! But don't go heading into your future just yet. Who can tell me the colour of their path to a fab future?* (This informs you how deeply involved they are in the visualisation.)

- *We're going to travel along this wonderful path! There's no need to say anything once we start. Just keep listening to what I'm saying, and enjoy zooming safely and happily along this path into your fab future.*

- *Close your eyes. Take three brilliant breaths. Ready, steady, go! Imagine that you are travelling very quickly but very quietly along the path to your future.*

- *See yourself zooming forward. Notice the bright **colours you see** as you speed along. Notice the **sparkly sounds you hear**. Notice how **good it feels** to head into your fab future.*

- *Now I want you to imagine that you have reached the time when you have just had your first day in your new class.*

- *Imagine you can stop and see yourself talking to someone at home about your first day in your new class! Yes, you can see yourself talking to someone at home!*

- *Now, remember that you are carrying your picture inside your hands. Hold your hands in front of you, and as we count down from five to one, imagine* *'beaming' your picture into your future. Keep your hands steady! Ready? Everyone help me count – **five, four, three, two, one**! Fantastic! What a fab future!*

- *As soon as you do this, you notice that your face is smiling as you talk to someone about your day.*

- *Notice that you can hear them saying 'Great!'*

- *Notice that you feel really good about the first day in your new class! Fantastic!*

- *And most important of all, notice that you will find yourself taking action to help you to reach this fab future.*

- *Now I'd like you to easily and happily fly back to right now. Take three more brilliant breaths and breathe in this really good feeling of change.*

- *Now open your eyes. Wow! Well done for taking action to create a more supportive view of the future.*

- This is a good time to share some of the actions they will take to move towards a fab future.

- As with Seeing Success, this strategy does not of course guarantee that their future will be just as they imagined, but it can go a long way towards empowering us to follow our dreams and risk enjoying a fab future.

LEAD DRIVER

'Flexibility opens opportunities!' – Fab Future is inherently about flexibility and creating opportunities. It encourages us to creatively consider our future and adapt our actions to achieve the goals we have set ourselves.

WHEN SHOULD I USE IT?

Children at Home (Examples)

You might use it when your child:

- Is worried about going to a new school
- Is anxious about a new brother or sister
- Is worried about a future test

Children at School (Examples)

You might use it when children:

- Face a big change
- Would benefit from the opportunity to think very creatively
- Need to consider action to achieve their goals

RELATED ACTIVITIES AT HOME

1. Have fun sharing Fab Future, especially imagining yourselves 'zooming along' together.
2. Share ideas about what the 'path to the future' looks like.
3. Talk with your child about how she or he views the future. What are they excited about? What are they anxious about? What could you both do to help relieve any anxiety?

RELATED ACTIVITIES AT SCHOOL

1. Discuss the experience with the children. What was it like zooming into the future? If any children found it hard to imagine, remind them that there's no success or failure with this. It's simply that the more they practice and enjoy themselves, the easier this can become.
2. Create a display of a future path and insert the changes the children have made.
3. Re-visit their future path at a later date and identify the goals achieved and the ones still to happen.

I JUST WONDERED...

Now you can see a path to your future, what is the first step you will take to make your goals actually happen?

SOMETHING TO CONSIDER - HOW MANY FROGS?

In many ways, identifying a goal is the easy part. It's taking the action to achieve that goal that is the difference between it simply being a 'nice idea' and becoming a reality. There is a lovely metaphor about twenty-nine frogs who sat by a pool and nine decided to jump in.

So how many were left on the side of the pool?

The answer is twenty-nine! The nine frogs had *decided* to jump in – but they didn't actually do it!

Eye of the Storm

Experiencing stillness

"Know thyself." – Socrates

WHAT IS IT?

Eye of the Storm is designed for children who show a certain maturity and self awareness. For example, they concentrate comfortably or they are able to positively influence their own emotional state, but they would benefit from opportunities to be even more focussed. Eye of the Storm aims to help them develop a deeper level of self awareness. It encourages children to access a state that can help them to gain distance from distractions, to be more reflective in their choices, and consequently to be more able to deal with challenges. This tool is about experiencing the calm in the very centre of the 'storm'. Locating and nurturing a sense of balance in the middle of the ups and downs.

WHY IS THIS IMPORTANT?

- The ability to experience calm when under pressure can be a real challenge, but can bring huge rewards in terms of dealing effectively with challenges and enjoying success.

- Eye of the Storm can support some of the key skills that enable success, problem-solving and excellence – for example, concentration, creativity and contemplation.
- Eye of the Storm can unlock some powerful creative imagery if children choose to describe their experiences.
- The power of silence and stillness can be a revelation for some children who lead hectic fast-paced lives.

HOW DO YOU DO IT?
(Resources: Relaxing calm background music if available)

Eye of the Storm – Summary

1. Begin Brilliant Breathing and notice your level of relaxation.
2. Imagine that all your thoughts are racing around your head.
3. Let them spin faster and faster and add colours, sounds and feelings.
4. They are all spinning around, but you find yourself at the very centre where it is calm, slow and very relaxed.
5. You watch as the spinning moves further and further away from you.
6. Using Brilliant Breathing as a focus, allow calm relaxation to circulate all around your body.
7. Focus on an inner sense of calm (the Eye of the Storm).
8. Emphasise that they do not need to struggle to find calm! Calm will naturally appear when we find balance.
9. Relax, reflect and re-energise.
10. Share experiences if they wish to do so, emphasising that there is no success or failure with this. The more you practice, the easier it becomes.

REACTIONS FROM CHILDREN WHEN USING EYE OF THE STORM

Sometimes children will tell you that aches, pains, headaches and so on, have diminished or gone completely after practising Eye of the Storm. They may have a very strong mind-body connection. Finding a quiet place within ourselves can sometimes have an even bigger impact than anticipated.

EYE OF THE STORM – THE SCRIPT

(Resources: Relaxing calm background music if available)
Specific Delivery Style: Very energised at first, becoming calmer, slower and quieter as the script moves from the 'storm' to 'calm'.

Remember what we do when we focus on success? Make sure your eyes are looking at me, you're listening very carefully and your body is nice and still. Let's begin...

- *Today we're going to use a tool called Eye of the Storm. Sounds exciting, doesn't it?*

- *Do you know that the Eye of the Storm is said to be the point right in the middle of a storm that is still and calm? Can you imagine that? A place right in the centre of a storm that is completely still and calm! That's what we're going to find today. But the storm isn't one with thunder, wind and rain – it's a whirlwind storm of all our thoughts.*

- *Are you ready for this? We begin a little differently. Instead of breathing deeply and looking for a relaxed calm place, I'd like you to think about your thoughts. In fact, I want you to imagine that your thoughts are racing around inside your head.*

- *Could you do that right now? I'd like you to close your eyes.*

- *Now, imagine hundreds of thoughts whirling around inside your head!*

- *These could be thoughts about how you are feeling, thoughts about what you did this morning, thoughts about what you want to do today, thoughts about what you will do later on, thoughts about friends, thoughts about school, thoughts about food, thoughts about television, thoughts about computer games, thoughts about tomorrow – a racing whirlwind of thoughts twisting and speeding inside your head!*

- *Now I'd like you to cover these thoughts with wonderful colours. Reds, blues, yellows, greens, golds – pour colours onto these thoughts as they race around inside your head. Add as many colours as you wish. Take a look at them right now – a whole rainbow of racing colours!*

- *Now add sounds to this whirlwind of colour. Loud sounds, sharp sounds, sudden sounds, hissing sounds, roaring sounds, surprising sounds. Add as many sounds as you wish. Listen to them right now.*

- *Now add feelings to this whirlwind of colour and sound. Feelings of speed, feelings of rushing, feelings of racing, feelings of whirling, feelings of spinning. Be aware of these feelings right now.*

- *Really notice all that you can see, hear and feel as these thoughts race around inside your head.*

- *And now I want you to breathe. In the middle of all these whirling colours, sounds and feelings I want you to begin slow deep breathing.*

- *As you breathe, notice that those rushing colours move further away from you.*

- *As you breathe, notice that those racing sounds move further away from you.*

- *As you breathe, notice that those rollercoaster feelings move further away from you.*

- *Notice that as you breathe you find yourself in the very middle of the rushing whirlwind, and it's incredibly still and quiet and relaxed.*

- *Notice that all those rushing whirling thoughts move even further away, and you find yourself slowing down completely.*

- *If you're trying really, really hard to find this calm, stop trying so hard! You don't need to struggle to find this stillness. It is always there, and it will become obvious when you choose to focus on the quietness inside.*

- *You find yourself breathing deeper, slower and really beginning to relax. Make this slowing down so obvious that I will be able to notice the difference just by looking at you.*

- *You find yourself in a really calm, still place, and you notice your relaxation getting stronger and stronger.*

- *Now allow this relaxing breath to move all the way around you, inside and outside.*

- *Allow this calm breath to flow around your legs, and then your body, and then your arms so that it's noticeable for you. You might even find that you feel warmer or cooler as you do this.*

- *Notice that all those rushing thoughts are still whirling around, but they are now so far away that you cannot hear them or feel them. You can just see a silent rainbow of colours way off in the distance.*

- *Choose to really notice how still you can become. Inside and outside. Smile to yourself as you breathe in silence and stillness.*

- *Now I'd like you to notice that you can send this calm feeling directly into your head. Do this right now. If any busy thoughts are left inside your head, allow this calm breath to gently nudge them away like a breeze brushing a cloud.*

- *Make your head as relaxed as you can. Breathe in space; breathe out thoughts. Make this so comfortable that you actually notice your own relaxation.*

- *If your inner voice is saying 'I can't do this', just let it drift away and enjoy what you can do.*

- *This is the Eye of the Storm. It is a very still and quiet space inside us. It is a place that is calm, a place that can leave us feeling relaxed, refreshed and re-energised. Ready to do whatever we need to do.*

- *It's the still place you experienced when you were content as a baby. It's the calm place you find just before you drift off to sleep. It's a sense of peace that seems like nothing at all, and yet brings a feeling of balance.*

- *Perhaps for you the Eye of the Storm is like the centre of a ripple on the water, or maybe like the silence in between the notes of a song, or maybe it's like the first sign of daylight in the morning.*

- *Remember, you don't have to struggle to find calm! When you let go of all those rushing thoughts, stillness will find you! It's always there, but often there is so much movement and noise and rushing around that it's easy to be distracted.*

- *Just let all the racing and rushing happen in the distance around you, while you enjoy this lovely still place.*

- *There's no success or failure attached to this. You won't feel the same as anyone else. You will feel how **you** feel.*

- *I'm going to let you focus for a while. Notice how still and quiet you can become. When you next hear my voice, take three nice slow brilliant breaths and then open your eyes. (Give them some time to focus on this experience.)*

- *Well done. You've chosen to learn how to slow down your thoughts and find a calm place within yourself.*

WHEN SHOULD I USE IT?

Children at Home (Examples)

You might use it when your child:

- Can confidently enjoy most of the tools from phase one and phase two and would benefit from a deeper level of relaxation and self awareness.
- Has a number of challenges to face and needs to find some space to avoid feeling overwhelmed.
- Enjoys experiencing quiet times.
  NB. If your child doesn't want to do Eye of the Storm, don't pursue it at this time. This would negate the positive relaxed focus of the activity.

CHILDREN AT SCHOOL (EXAMPLES)
You might use it when children:

- Often excel, but sometimes put themselves under too much pressure.
- Normally have high levels of concentration, but momentarily find it hard to focus.
- Are particularly skilful and confident and you wish to stretch their creativity and encourage even deeper self awareness.

RELATED ACTIVITIES AT HOME

1. Talk with your child about the 'racing whirlwind of thoughts' Do they ever experience this?
2. Talk about the images that your child experienced. Discuss how the colours, sounds or feelings link with different thoughts.
3. Discuss how your child felt before and after Eye of the Storm.

RELATED ACTIVITIES AT SCHOOL

1. Ask the children to share their experiences of the racing storm of thoughts and the still point in the centre. Ask what was it like when they chose to notice the silence and stillness inside themselves?
2. Ask the children to draw a picture of themselves in the middle of a racing storm of thoughts, and identify how they feel in the calm centre.
3. Create a display or model of the colourful 'storm of thoughts' with calm still images in the centre.

I JUST WONDERED...

If a lovely still calm place is actually inside of us, why don't we experience this more often?

SOMETHING TO CONSIDER – LEARNING AND EMOTIONS

We will all have experienced times when learning seems to flow and other times when we are too anxious to learn. There is a part of the brain called the limbic system which is thought to be the centre of our emotions. It is located between the brainstem and the cortex, and provides the link between our thoughts and our feelings. When the limbic system is overwhelmed with negative emotions, learning becomes virtually impossible. The tools within this book provide a structure for children to access a more positive emotional state, to support their ability to succeed.

Using the tools during the school day

Tools most suitable to use *before* the lesson

Ready 4 Learning Ladder: For when you want to check the children are motivated and ready to begin an activity.

The Smasher: For when you have children who have limiting self beliefs about their ability to complete an activity.

The Jacket: For when you want children to develop resilience when faced with setbacks.

Change Your Mind: For when you want to know how children 'see' a planned activity, especially if you think they have a picture in their heads of it not going well.

Enjoying Excellence: For when you want children to recognise achievements and to consider what choices and actions will help them to achieve excellence.

Tools most suitable *during* the lesson
(Once children are familiar with these tools they can use them independently during the lesson when required.)

Brilliant Breathing: For when you want to create a relaxed empowered state. This is especially useful when you are asking children to recall previous learning by attaining the 'alpha state.' (See Personal Space -*Something to Consider*).

My Choice of Inner Voice: For when individuals or groups are having 'problems'.

Personal Power: For when children need to feel more empowered during an activity.

Seeing Success: For when you want children to have the tenacity to see a task through to the end.

Shield: For when you want children to share their outcomes but some feel reticent to do so.

Tools most suitable *after* a lesson

Shrink: For when an activity didn't go well and children feel a negative emotion.

Personal Space: For when you want all the children to relax, reflect and re-energise after a lesson.

Fab Future: For when you want the children to consider the impact of what they've achieved.

Step Forward: For when you want the children to feel connected to a future goal.

Eye of the Storm (for more experienced children): For when you want children to feel a sense of inner calm and balance.

NB: Obviously these are simply guidelines and you are encouraged to use any of the tools to match your requirements at any given time.

USING THE TOOLS FOR SUCCESS WITH PARTICULAR THEMES

Overleaf are some introductory guidelines with ideas for how the tools might be linked with particular issues or challenges. As you become familiar with them, adapt and extend them to meet your specific needs.

Each theme identifies some of the positive behaviours we might exhibit i.e. *'in rapport'*, or some of the negative behaviours i.e. *'out of rapport.'*

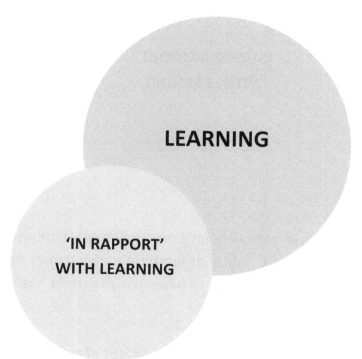

Being in rapport with learning can be the deciding factor in how successfully children undertake any activity. Being 'in rapport' with learning includes feeling curious, confident and appropriately challenged.

Some of the 'signs and symptoms' of being 'in rapport' with issues around learning can include:

- The ability to make mistakes, learn from them and have another go
- The ability to recognise, appreciate and share successes
- The ability to maintain concentration and be interested
- The ability to be physically relaxed while learning
- The ability to self motivate
- The ability to enjoy learning

LEARNING

'OUT OF RAPPORT' WITH LEARNING

All children will have experienced times when learning seems to flow — for example, learning a new hobby or learning a new game. However, there are also times when learning seems to have many barriers. I refer to this as being 'out of rapport' with learning.

Some of the 'signs and symptoms' of being 'out of rapport' with issues around learning can include:

- Feeling nervous when asked to begin a new activity
- Expecting it all to go wrong
- 'Seeing' everyone else succeeding
- Feeling physically unwell
- Feeling it's a 'fluke' when something goes right
- Waiting to be discovered! — fearing that others will find out that you're not that 'clever'

TOOLS THAT ARE PARTICULARLY USEFUL FOR ADDRESSING ISSUES AROUND LEARNING

Brilliant Breathing p.21 — Accessing a more relaxed state that can help children to recall information

My Choice of Inner Voice p.34 — Creating a Power Statement that refutes 'I'm stupid'!

Ready 4 Learning Ladder p.27 — Taking control of my motivation to learn

The Jacket p.83 — Recognising, appreciating and building on achievements

Enjoying Excellence p.107 — Making sure children know how to find excellence within themselves

---

BULLYING

'IN RAPPORT' WITH BULLYING-RELATED ISSUES

Being 'in rapport' with bullying is when children recognise the inappropriateness of bullying and would do their best to take action if bullying occurred.

Some of the 'signs and symptoms' of being 'in rapport' with issues around bullying can include:

- The ability to recognise bullying
- The ability to ignore peer pressure that encourages bullying
- The ability to speak to an adult when bullying has occurred
- The ability to understand that it is not easy to take action against a bully
- The ability to forgive themselves when they are too fearful to take action, e.g. to tell an adult
- The ability to recognise that the fault is with the bully and not with themselves

BULLYING

'OUT OF RAPPORT' WITH BULLYING-RELATED ISSUES

Feeling 'out of rapport' with bullying can have a major impact on children, and can take many forms.

Some of the 'signs and symptoms' of being 'out of rapport' with issues around bullying, *especially for children being bullied*, can include:

- Blaming themselves
- Believing it will never end
- Feeling that no one else could understand
- Expecting bullying to take place
- School refusal or frequent 'illness'
- Finding it difficult to trust
- Feeling that nothing can be done

TOOLS THAT ARE PARTICULARLY USEFUL FOR ADDRESSING ISSUES AROUND BULLYING

My Choice of Inner Voice p.34 – Replacing the inner voice that says 'Nobody can help me!'

Personal Power p.40 – Creating a feeling of empowerment for someone who has been bullied

Seeing Success p.63 – 'Seeing' yourself having the confidence to tell someone

The Jacket p.83 – Recognising the qualities we have that remind us we can succeed against bullying

The Smasher p.46 – A child who is being bullied may use The Smasher to destroy a 'wall' that depicts an inappropriate belief – for example, 'It must be my fault!'

ANGER

'IN RAPPORT' WITH ANGER-RELATED ISSUES

Being 'in rapport' with anger can allow us to feel and express anger without completely 'losing ourselves'. It means being aware of triggers, feeling anger when it is appropriate, and taking action that is appropriate.

Some of the 'signs and symptoms' of being 'in rapport' with issues around anger can include:

- The ability to control anger rather than take it out on those around them
- The ability to use supportive strategies to 'let go' of anger
- The ability to recognise the triggers for anger that they possess (*the first signs*)
- The ability to release anger appropriately
- The ability to know when their response has been inappropriate, and to learn from this

ANGER

'OUT OF RAPPORT' WITH ANGER-RELATED ISSUES

There will be times when children feel anger and it is the appropriate feeling to have. It is how they react to this feeling that is important. All children will have had times when they have felt inappropriate anger. If this happens on a regular basis, this can be a key sign of being 'out of rapport' with anger.

Some of the 'signs and symptoms' of being 'out of rapport' with issues around anger can include:

- Being 'experts' at losing their tempers
- Frequently experiencing anger inside themselves even though they don't show it to others *(which can lead to various stress-related symptoms)*
- Always needing to apologise
- Regularly feeling angry with others or themselves
- Unable to relax or feel sustained joy
- *Possible* bullying tendencies

TOOLS THAT ARE PARTICULARLY USEFUL FOR ADDRESSING ISSUES AROUND ANGER

Brilliant Breathing p.21 – Creating a new response pattern by breathing to calm down

Shrink p.70 – Giving 'anger' or 'my temper' a tangible form that can allow children to begin to initiate changes, rather than the anger taking control of them

Personal Space p.76 – Enjoying a sustained sense of calm

Fab Future p.114 – Using visualisation to see, hear and feel ourselves effectively dealing with anger in the future

Eye of the Storm p.121 – Letting go of the 'inner storm' and experiencing calm

---

FRIENDSHIPS

'IN RAPPORT' WITH FRIENDSHIP-RELATED ISSUES

Being 'in rapport' with others and comfortable with friendship groups is essential for relating to peers and not feeling threatened by complex social dynamics.

Some of the 'signs and symptoms' of being 'in rapport' with issues around friendship can include:

- The ability to confidently initiate a friendship
- The ability to re-establish a friendship after a disagreement
- The ability to listen and hear
- The ability to accurately interpret non-verbal communication
- The ability to empathise and show care towards others
- The ability to put forward a viewpoint firmly but not aggressively
- The ability to laugh and have fun

FRIENDSHIPS

'OUT OF RAPPORT' WITH FRIENDSHIP-RELATED ISSUES

All children feel 'out of rapport' with others at different times in their lives, but if this is a regular experience it can lead to loss of confidence or isolation.

Some of the 'signs and symptoms' of being 'out of rapport' with issues around friendship can include:

- Feeling left out of groups
- Expecting others to talk about them behind their backs
- Feeling threatened in social situations
- Feeling anxious about school
- Refusing to attend parties or social functions
- Self isolation because it feels safer
- Saying the 'wrong thing' because of misreading non-verbal communications

---

TOOLS THAT ARE PARTICULARLY USEFUL FOR ADDRESSING ISSUES AROUND FRIENDSHIPS

Personal Power p.40 – Giving themselves the confidence to initiate friendships

Seeing Success p.63 – Helping children to envisage a positive social event

Shrink p.70 – Helping children to let go of negative feelings relating to friendships – e.g 'I'm too nervous' or 'I'm too shy'

Step Forward p.101 – Embedding strong links with an empowering goal that supports friendships

Enjoying Excellence p.107 – An opportunity to consider what excellence in 'friendships' means

---

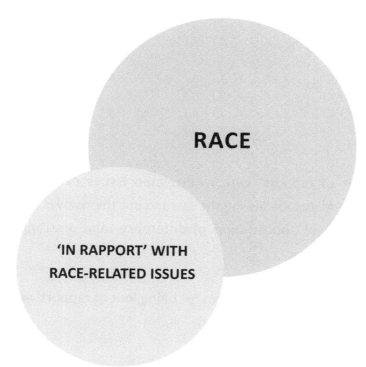

RACE

'IN RAPPORT' WITH RACE-RELATED ISSUES

Being 'in rapport' with race-related issues includes having positive self belief, a sincere appreciation of difference, and the skills and confidence to appropriately challenge issues that are unjust or discriminatory.

Some of the 'signs and symptoms' of being 'in rapport' with issues around race can include:

- A pride in one's own ethnicity combined with a respect for the ethnicity of others
- A real interest in finding out about other cultures, beliefs, traditions and so on
- An ability to recognise and challenge racist comments or behaviour
- Understanding that difference is a strength not a weakness

RACE

'OUT OF RAPPORT' WITH
RACE-RELATED ISSUES

Feeling 'out of rapport' with race-related issues can have a major impact on individuals, and include feeling the need to put themselves 'above' another group or culture, a lack of appreciation of difference, and a strong opposition to other viewpoints.

Some of the 'signs and symptoms' of being 'out of rapport' with issues around race can include:

- Believing that difference is threatening
- Generalisations about groups of people
- Lack of self awareness and empathy
- Beliefs based upon stereotypes
- Low self esteem, resulting in a need to identify 'inferior' groups or cultures

---

TOOLS THAT ARE PARTICULARLY USEFUL
FOR ADDRESSING ISSUES AROUND RACE

The Smasher p.46 – A child who has faced racism smashing a wall that says 'Nothing can be done'

Personal Power p.40 – Creating a feeling of empowerment for someone who has experienced racism

My Choice of Inner Voice p.34 – Creating a power statement that challenges racist attitudes

Fab Future p.114 – Embedding powerful goals that encourage aspiration

Eye of the Storm p.121 – Letting go of negative thoughts and finding balance

---

Quantum Questions

Powerful questioning is one of the keys to challenging our perceptions, unlocking barriers and allowing us to exceed expectations. There are some styles of questioning that challenge our fundamental viewpoint and encourage us to take a 'quantum leap of perspective'. I call these 'Quantum Questions'. They are not intended to question the validity of a state or to undermine a feeling, but they do present new possibilities. **Some questions deliberately combine past, present or future tenses.** This technique can help to displace the structure we have placed around a belief. Simply puzzling over these questions and giving them serious reflection can be enough of a catalyst to consider a new way forward (and to locate the exit of 'the red box'.)

1. I know you feel you don't know what to do, but what would you do if you did know?
2. How did you stop yourself doing well in the past, and what do you now do differently?
3. How will this challenge inevitably lead to something so much better?
4. How do you do "I'm not successful?" How hard do you work every single day to keep this belief really strong?
5. If you looked back at yourself next week and you are definitely successful, what would be different?
6. If this problem is actually the solution you've been waiting for, what would be different?
7. If success was shadowing you each and every day, how will you know?
8. If you were your own best friend, what sentence would you say to yourself that would turn everything around?
9. If you couldn't fail, how could you stop yourself succeeding?
10. If you were just told some incredible news about something that has nothing to do with this problem, what would happen to the problem?

*By the way – is your inner voice helping you or getting in your way right **now**?*

Guidelines for sharing the tools with your child

SHARING THE ACTIVITES AT HOME
- **Enjoy having time together and sharing the questions.**
- **If your child is happy to talk to you about the tools – great!**
- **If your child just wants to listen, then share your thoughts about the tool.**
- **If your child doesn't want to do it at all, no problem. Do it another day.**
- **Once children realise this is a special time to have with a special adult, they will often look forward to it.**
- **Try to maintain a positive response to whatever they say. This is all about success.**
- **If you're not sure how to respond, have a quiet word with your child's teacher to see if they have any advice.**

READING A SCRIPT

- **First of all, make yourself a hot drink, relax and read through the *'Guide for sharing the scripts'* (p.10)**
- **Next, read the relevant pages about the particular tool you want to use.**
- **Don't be worried about 'how good' you will be at reading the script.**
- **Don't be worried if you're interrupted or it doesn't go to plan. Try again another time. Flexibility is key.**
- **As you gain confidence, change the scripts to meet your needs. Enjoy!**

NB If your inner voice says 'I won't be any good at this!', change it for a Power Statement – for example, 'I can do my best!'

Adults enjoying success for themselves!

One of the very best ways to influence children is to model the behaviour you are asking them to adopt. So what about your success? All the approaches in this book have been used to support the success of adults as well as children.

GROUP SUPPORT

One of the most powerful and fun ways to use the tools is to ask a close friend or a group of friends to share the scripts together. This can become a very supportive network. Use tools that you feel comfortable sharing, and feel free to amend and adapt the words to match your needs.

The tools most frequently used by adults

Brilliant Breathing – Changing our state through breathing (often a useful one to begin an adult session)

Many people state that they haven't even got time to breathe! Life seems to be getting faster and faster. Brilliant Breathing addresses this by making us focus on **this** particular moment and slowing right down. Having a strategy for letting go of tensions and focussing on empowerment has obvious potential benefits for all of us.

My Choice of Inner Voice – Taking control of the inner voice

Having an opportunity to influence those internal conversations can be a huge relief. We know how these solo interactions can delete any of the positive qualities we possess and frequently make us focus on the negative.

Personal Power – Creating inner strength and confidence

As a leader, teacher, parent or carer you will be constantly 'giving out'. This can make us feel emotionally drained and unable to deal effectively with some of the challenges we face. Giving yourself time to re-energise and creating a feeling of resourcefulness can be critical in sustaining long-term success.

Seeing Success – Being drawn towards a positive outcome

We all face constant new challenges that can generate doubts and concerns. This can sometimes make us view the future with trepidation. Seeing Success makes us focus on a more positive perspective and helps us change our expectations. A great deal of research has shown that expectations can play a key part in future outcomes, especially with children.

The Jacket – Recognising strengths

It is easy for adults to delete the many qualities we possess. This tool forces us to consider our strengths, and this can give us the confidence to address any areas where we might need support as a teacher, parent or carer. This tool is especially powerful when shared with friends because they will be able to recognise and appreciate many of our qualities that we delete. *(Adults frequently use this tool to support preparation for job interviews.)*

Eye of the Storm – Letting go of invasive thoughts and feeling calm

This tool provides a creative structure for letting go of the thoughts that can accompany us throughout the day. It is easy for adults to lose themselves during a day when they are giving out so much. Eye of the Storm addresses this by creating a sense of balance and calm right in the middle of all the daily pressures. It can be a powerful catalyst for re-assessing priorities and finding our sense of self.

Step Forward – Moving towards a powerful goal

This tool can provide adults with a framework for feeling connected to a goal, for example, to change careers; to make a lifestyle change; to learn a new skill and so on. When Step Forward is shared with a supportive group of friends or colleagues, it can greatly increase camaraderie, aspiration, and the motivation to succeed.

Personal Space – Having time for me!

A powerful way to end an adult session is to use the Personal Space script. With the hectic lives we lead, finding quality time for ourselves is often out of the question. This longer relaxation script can encourage an even deeper experience of the three Rs – reflecting, relaxing and re-energising.

Relevant drivers for adults who are using the tools themselves

We become experts at whatever we practice: The more we enjoy these tools, the more confident we will feel in using and adapting them.

Success is within us and is always an option: A useful message to ourselves if we're worried about *failing*!

Mistakes are magnificent when they lead to learning: This means we can't fail! We simply realise that each *mistake* is actually useful feedback.

Rapport with others is very important. Rapport with ourselves is essential: Appreciate the time with friends, and congratulate yourself for choosing to give yourself time. You deserve it!

The magic is in *this* moment: Take the time to slow things down and really notice what you see, hear and feel during the session. Whenever your mind wanders, simply come back to Brilliant Breathing and enjoy.

In conclusion:

I hope that using Success in Schools is a unique and positive experience for you and your child, or the children you work with.

Many adults have never been given strategies to respond to the fundamental issues explored in this book. These issues impact on every aspect of success. It is up to us to give children as many ways as possible to respond powerfully to the challenges they will face.

This is what I call 'self acuity' – when children effectively manage their own states, respect themselves and others, and have the confidence, ability and tenacity to happily seek success in all its diverse forms.

Bibliography

Use Your Head, Tony Buzan, BBC Worldwide Limited, London, 2000

Dynamic Learning, Robert Dilts and Todd Epstein, Meta Publications, Capitola CA 1995

The Brain that Changes Itself, Norman Doidge, Penguin, London, 2008

Bullying: A Practical Guide to Coping for Schools, Michele Elliott, Pearson Education London, 1997

Emotional Intelligence, Daniel Goleman, Bloomsbury Publishing, London, 1996

Working with Emotional Intelligence, Daniel Goleman, Bloomsbury Publishing, London, 1999

How Your Mind Can Heal Your Body, David R. Hamilton, Hay House, London, 2008

The Contagious Power of Thinking, David R. Hamilton, Hay House, London, 2011

Starting from the Child: Teaching and Learning in the Foundation Stage, Julie Fisher, McGraw Hill, Maidenhead, 2008

Beginning Teaching: Beginning Learning, Janet Moyles, OUP, *Buckingham:1995*

The NLP Coach, Ian McDermott and Wendy Jago, Piatkus Books, London, 2002

NLP Business Masterclass, David Molden, Pearson Education Ltd, Harlow, 2007

Molecules of Emotion, Candace Pert, Pocket Books, London, 1999